Survivor Song

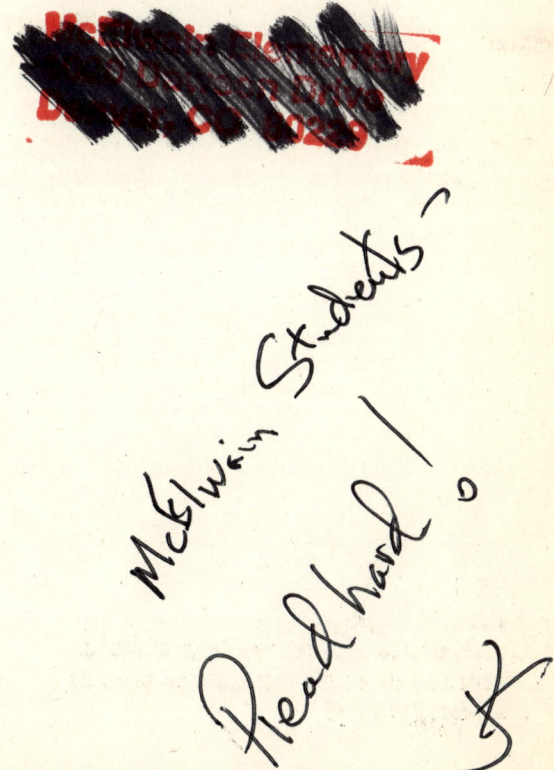

McElwain Students ~

Read hard!

Also by Joseph Kehoe

They're Coming For You:
Scary Stories that Scream to be Read

Survivor Song

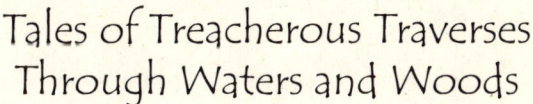

Tales of Treacherous Traverses
Through Waters and Woods

by
Joseph Kehoe

You Come Too Publishing

Survivor Song: *Tales of Treacherous Traverses Through Waters and Woods*
Published by You Come Too Publishing, Bend, Oregon.

Copyright © 2009 by Joseph Kehoe.

Printed in the United States of America
First edition, 2009

Publisher's Cataloging-in-Publication
Kehoe, Joseph
Survivor song : tales of treacherous traverses
through waters and woods / written by Joseph Kehoe
p. cm.
SUMMARY: This collection of gritty, suspenseful, survival stories set in the North American wilderness include kayaking, canoeing, hiking, and snowshoeing. Characters include a lost kayaker who makes a horrible discovery, a young man who races against the merciless desert sun to save his father, and a girl in a battle of life and death after her training run in the snowy forest goes terribly wrong.
Audience: Ages 9-12.
LCCN 2009924554
ISBN-13: 978-0-9816836-1-4
ISBN-10: 0-9816836-1-4
1. Wilderness survival--North America--Juvenile fiction.
2. Children's stories, American. 3. Adventure stories, American.
[1. Wilderness survival--North America--Fiction.
2. Wilderness areas--North America--Fiction. 3. Adventure and adventurers--Fiction.]   I. Title.
PZ7.P384485Tal 2009
[Fic] QBI09-600029

For my huckleberry friend

Contents

~~~~~~

Dance
of the Boiled Brains

Craig could always tell when his father had been drinking. His eyes would get small and distant. His mouth would become small too. But mostly he would get quiet.

The car was engulfed in that drinking quiet now as it sped along at more than 90 miles an hour through the Utah desert.

It never quite felt like fun to Craig, not the way his friends made it sound at school talking about their favorite racecar drivers. He wasn't afraid of crashing–it just felt wrong. His father never seemed to enjoy going fast either. The more he drank, the harder he pressed his foot down on the accelerator. That's all there was to it.

It was like a mathematical equation. Fun had nothing to do with it.

As the desert blurred by on all sides, Craig looked at the bug splatters on the windshield and tried to think about the hike ahead. They were headed for Canyonlands National Park. It was going to be his last camping trip before starting middle school back in Phoenix.

When they reached the trailhead, Craig strapped on the heavy, old-fashioned, external-frame backpack. One time a passing hiker had asked him if he had stolen it from a museum. It was a real relic all right, but it got the job done.

Since there was little chance of finding drinkable water along the way, they had to bring their own. They were supposed to be out for two days. The formula was one gallon per person per day. That meant four gallons. And each gallon weighed about eight pounds.

Craig wasn't happy about having to haul the extra weight in addition to his gear, but he didn't complain. He knew his father's pack weighed even more.

The miles passed quickly as they descended the canyon in silence. Except for the strain of the pack and the heat, it was easy hiking. Late August in this desert was too uncomfortable for most hikers, and that's the way his father liked it. Fewer people. One of the reasons for coming out here was to get away from people, he would say.

Craig had grown up in the desert and didn't use the word lightly like a tourist or some dried-up blue hair. But today was going to be one *hot* mother. Big, black ravens called down to them from their shady perch high above the trail.

"Don't look at them in the eyes," Craig's grand-mother warned him once. "Those birds are evil."

As Craig drank from his water bottle on an overlook by the side of the trail, he saw his father sneak a quick drink, the sun mirroring off the silver flask.

He wished it could be different. Sometimes it was. Sometimes it was good. It was good when his father didn't drink. It was good and the world was a special place. A place full of eye-rubbing relief and sweetness and even a kind of quiet joy.

While Craig looked at the towering formations in the distance, his father stepped too close to the edge. He heard the rocks start to give way and turned in time to see him fall silently, disappearing in a flurry of dirt and sand.

"Dad!" Craig shouted. "Dad!"

He scrambled down toward the broken figure far below. Long before reaching him, Craig could tell something was seriously wrong. His father's lower leg was bent in a terrible way. A bone in his calf was trying to poke out through the skin. The leg immediately started to swell, turning a sickly shade of purple. His father moaned and shivered in the late morning heat.

As his heart raced, Craig knew he had to get help. He hated the idea of leaving his father, but there was no time to waste. Craig covered him with a windbreaker, left his pack and most of the water, and kissed his father on the forehead.

"I'm going for help," he said. "Drink the water."

He scrambled back up to the trail, twice losing his balance and almost falling. He looked down but couldn't see his father. He built a cairn in the middle of the trail to mark the spot and yelled down.

"I'll be back!"

The air was now blow-dryer hot and the trail would be uphill all the way back to the car. Craig wasn't sure how long they had been hiking when the accident happened, but it seemed he was much closer to the canyon bottom than to the rim. He had a long way to go. But freed from the weight of the pack and fueled by the concern he felt for his father, he made quick progress.

After a while Craig stopped under the shade of a rocky overhang to catch his breath and drink some water. He remembered learning in school about an explorer named Cabrillo who had died off the coast of California after breaking his leg. Craig wondered how such a thing could be possible. Kids and athletes broke their arms and legs all the time. But he had never heard of any of them dying. How could someone die from a broken leg? But picturing the ugly purple bulge sticking out from his father, he didn't have to use too much imagination to see how it might begin to be possible. He tried to think of something else.

When he was younger, Craig thought he had the power to keep his father from drinking. He thought that if he was especially good that day, that his father would come home sober. Eventually he came to the slow, sad realization that there was no connection. It didn't matter what he did. Hard as he tried, Craig couldn't keep his father from getting fired from another job or from passing out somewhere and never making it home.

"Caw! Caw! Caw!"

The raven's loud, sudden scream surprised Craig so much, he lost his grip on the water bottle. He stabbed at it in midair but only managed to bat it down a long stretch of slickrock. The precious liquid emptied into the sand far below while Craig shook his fist at the bird.

"Son of a . . . " he shouted as he looked for a rock to throw at the raven. But what good would that do? "Ah, I don't have time for this."

He started walking again but soon began to feel strange, disconnected from his thoughts. His pace slowed down. His cheeks felt hotter than when Mrs. Clelia called on him and he didn't know the answer. Mirage-like swirls of air danced above the baking brown and red rocks. He was swimming in an ocean of sweat and thinking about Cabrillo and his leg and thinking about his father. So many one-legged pirates. *Arrr.* Would his father lose his leg too?

Hard to dance on one leg. Even so, Cabrillo was now dancing on the water. Dancing like a cardboard cutout of Jonathan Papelbon, Craig's favorite pitcher. A pitcher of ice water. He would drink it all in one gulp. He could almost taste it. All in one gulp. No, better leave some for Cabrillo. As easy as he was making it look, dancing on water still had to make a man mighty thirsty.

Craig remembered one of his father's favorite songs. Something about how doing nothing can still make you very thirsty. The music played in his head as he grappled with the lyrics. *Mmm, mmm, something, something, mean, mean thirst . . .* Whatever. Anyway Cabrillo and I are certainly not doing nothing, he thought.

"Not doing *anything*," his teacher corrected.

"Get lost, Mrs. Clelia!" Craig shouted as she disappeared into the sand.

Thirsty. Climbing across a furnace of sandstone and sand and stone and more sandstone. So thirsty.

Papelbon would spray champagne around the field like a madman after a big Red Sox victory. And he would dance. He would dance a crazy little Irish jig. Craig's mind was doing a jig of its own now. Dancing in and out of reality.

Glowing, fiery ball 93 million miles away scorching Craig's skin, singeing his soul. Climbing, climbing thousands of feet. No one else on the trail. No one else stupid enough, Craig thought. Must keep climbing through this desert of stupidity. All was quiet. The ravens must be taking naps.

The terrible, haunting quiet between the time his father would close the car door and reach the front door. Maybe he wouldn't be drunk this time. Maybe he . . . and then he walked in, killing all doubt. The house was filled with silence again and disappointment and, for Craig, just a little heartbreak. His younger sister was too little to understand a lot of what went on. And his mother was too tired from working so hard at two jobs and from working so hard at keeping the family going to feel much more than exhaustion.

Back here now. Sand. Rocks. Four-letter word for inferno. Starts with an *h*. Not a creature was stirring, not even a . . . lizard. Craig laughed. That was a good one. But it wasn't anywhere near Christmas. No presents today. No water under the tree. No tree. Not a Christmas tree as far as the eye could see. Just rocks and brush and rocks and shrubs and rocks and . . . Cabrillo meeting the natives.

"Hell-Oh, Natives. Got any gold? I will dance on the water for you. Watch me dance. Miren como bailo!"

Hot. So hot. Leaden boots on molten gold. Rocks. Why aren't the rocks melting? Cabrillo saying something. What?

"Las piedras marcan el lugar. Las piedras marcan el lugar."

"Cabrillo!" Craig called out. "I don't speak Spanish."

17

The ever-shrinking, thinking part of his brain knew he should get out of the sun, and under normal circumstances he would. But these weren't normal circumstances. These were extreme leg-bending-the-wrong-freakin'-way circumstances.

Stomach not feeling so good now. Craig hated vomiting. Even though he knew he would feel better if he just let it fly, he would always hold it down as long as he could. Once he waited several hours for his mom to come home from work so she could stroke his hair as he leaned over the toilet bowl.

But his mom wasn't here now. Craig stumbled over behind a boulder and brought up what remained of his breakfast on the ground between his feet. He could make out the poppy seeds in the soggy muffin chunks as they began to soak into the red dirt. A lizard scurried under a rock. And as always, Craig felt a little better.

He wiped his mouth and got back on the trail. He had to be close. Closer at least.

"*Take us with you!*" the muffin chunks yelled behind him. "*Don't leave us here!*"

"Maybe next time," Craig mumbled. He wasn't worried anymore. Wasn't sweating anymore. Wasn't thirsty anymore. Everything seemed to be golden and shining and nothing mattered. It would be okay to rest for a little while. To sit down in the shade and wait for Cabrillo to sail by. For Papelbon to come in from the bullpen and save the game . . .

"These are great seats," Craig said to his father as he smiled and sipped on a large Coke. "I always wanted to see a game from the top of the Green Monster."

Big Papi up to bat. He fouls one back and breaks his bat. Wait. That's not a bat. It's a leg. Big Papi's holding a broken leg. A twisted, shattered leg with a jagged white bone sticking through . . .

No! Must keep going. Must get help. Get help. Take one step. Then another. Keep moving. Up the trail. Get help. Help up there. Father down there. Hurt. Up there. Help.

The sun had gone down behind the canyon rim. But it had done its damage.

What was left of Craig was moving very slowly now, barely making any progress at all. Toward the end, he was walking like his father did when he had had too much to drink. He didn't think about what he would do if there wasn't anyone at the top. Didn't think. Couldn't think.

At some point, Craig stumbled into the parking lot and saw Papelbon and his pretty wife getting out of their car.

"Help," he yelled but it only came out as a whisper. "Help."

He took another step toward them and collapsed.

"We need to call for help," he heard the woman say as she knelt over him. "Get him some water."

"Drink this, kid," *Papelbon* said, spraying Craig with champagne. His eyes stung as he drank deeply.

"Papelbon, Papelbon," Craig pleaded, tugging on the man's sleeve and pointing down the trail. "Cabrillo . . . my dad . . . *pierna quebrada* . . . leg . . . needs help. Help him, Papelbon."

"This kid's nuts," the man said. "What's he talking about? And why's he calling me *Papelbon*?"

***

Later, as they rode in the speeding ambulance, Craig caught something in his father's pained, red eyes. He knew it was as close as his father would–or could–come to apologizing. And then he looked away.

Craig was glad he didn't promise that it would never happen again. That this would be the last time. That he would stop drinking. Craig was getting too old for those no-leg-to-stand-on promises that never amounted to anything.

He squeezed his father's arm and looked off in the distance, sipping slowly from a water bottle. They rode in silence all the way to the hospital.

Angel

"I would not go that way if I were you," Victor said.

"This is the way, Vicky. I told you I've been here before," Angel said, looking past the snow at the trail on the other side. "*Andale, carnal.*"

Stalling, Victor drank slowly from his water bottle. It was dusty and hot, even for July, on the steep path that led to the summit of Mt. Tallac. But it was not quite hot enough to melt this patch of snow.

Veronica, Victor's sister, had driven them to the trailhead and would pick them up after her shift ended at the casino on the Nevada side of the state line with California. When they had left, the sun was just coming up. It had been hard getting up so early, but Victor was glad to be spending the day with Angel. Despite what his mom said, Angel was good people. You just had to get to know him.

"*Ese va a terminar mal,*" she told him often. "Make sure you think for yourself when you're out with him, *m'hijo*. Just a matter of time with that one."

All Victor knew was that Angel was his best friend. Yeah, he had a little problem with authority and sometimes he would make some of those bad choices the adults were always warning against. But he had another side too, a side most people didn't see.

"Man, it drops a long way if we slip," Victor said, looking at the rocky precipice. It was hundreds of feet down, maybe even a thousand. The scavengers would have a dead man's party on what was left.

"You always show up with that fear of yours. Everywhere we go," Angel said. "C'mon now, girl, this is the way."

This was the Angel adults knew. The bully. The pusher. Always pushing things too far. The Angel who set fire to his sister's dress–while she was still wearing it. The Angel who broke into the school with some older boys one Sunday in 5th grade and clogged the toilets with paper towels and stole stuff from the teachers' desks.

"School's better when nobody's there," he said, bragging to Victor when the principal finally let him back in. "Nobody tells you what to do."

Victor liked the Angel who spent Saturday afternoons with him by a lake catching trout or playing soccer in the park using trash cans to mark the goals because the *gringos* locked up the real ones.

"Do they think we're going to steal them or something?" Angel would say, beginning to get mad. "Or maybe use the net to go fishing?"

But then he would drive a shot low and hard off the can and into the *goal* and start laughing. Laughing as if laughing were his sole purpose in life.

At those times–when the hardness left him–Angel was good to be around. At those times, Victor could tell him about the terrible yelling between his parents that tore through the house on the weekends and about how sometimes his father wouldn't come home at night.

"Man, that sucks," Angel would say. "No worries, holmes, I got your back."

Victor was worried about his back right now, along with all his other parts. They had hiked for almost three hours and were close to cresting the top of the final ridge. But suddenly the path was leading them across this small 30-foot patch of snow. If they slipped, it wouldn't be pretty. It would be downright nasty.

"This is crazy," Victor said.

"Have some faith, bro," Angel said.

The two boys actually were like brothers, Victor thought. Same schools and classes since kindergarten. They hadn't done too much hiking in the past, but this summer they were hitting the trails two or three times a week. It was good to be away from the house and their parents and to be outside in the Sierra Nevada summer. It felt good to do something physical too, to feel the old muscles come back alongside new ones. The elevation gain was more than 3000 feet on this 10-mile hike, just the way they liked it. A good workout. None of that flatliner stuff.

"I'm so bulked up and ripped since when we left school, man," Victor had said to Angel on their first water break as the blazing sun climbed above the trees.

"Nah, *tu mamá* maybe, but not you."

Victor took off his backpack and slammed it into Angel's chest. They both laughed.

Victor couldn't stop thinking about his mother's advice now. He was sure that the first step on that icy snow would be a one-way ticket down a rocky oblivion.

"Angel, there's not even any footprints in the snow," he said. "No one's been through here. It can't be the trail."

"Let's eat something," Angel said, sounding a little disgusted.

They pulled back from the snow patch, back onto the safety of the dirt and dust. They looked off in opposite directions and ate their candy bars in silence.

"There must be another way," Victor said after a while. But even as he said it, he knew that

Angel had a death grip on it–this idea of crossing through the snow–and no way was he letting go. Victor couldn't ever remember a time when Angel backed down from anything. No matter the price or the pain, he would not give up on a thing.

"We're doing this," Angel said, drinking some water.

Victor's stomach sank, the chocolate and peanuts mixing with the now fear-flavored nougat.

The boys walked up to the edge of the snow again. It really wasn't that far across, maybe nine, ten steps to get back on dirt. But the snow reminded Victor of one of those crazy, icy slopes in that Grinch movie, super steep and slick.

"We'll walk fast. That'll help. Maybe run across," Angel said. "If you start slipping, throw your body forward. I'll go first so I can grab you if I need to."

Clearly, Angel had been watching too much James Bond, Victor thought.

"You've seen too much Bond, man," he said. "This is real."

"And you're *real*-ly making too much of it," Angel said. "Once we're through this, we're only about half an hour from the top. We're so close."

Suddenly someone walked up behind them.

"Man, don't sneak up like that," Angel said, losing his balance a little.

The tall man had long hair and a beard and carried a walking stick. Those walking sticks always made the boys laugh, selling for 50 bucks in town when you could find plenty of sticks in the woods for free.

"There's a better way up over here," he said.

"Nah, we got it, man. Thanks anyway," Angel said.

"No, really. It's right here. You just passed the trail," the man said. "It'll be a lot faster and you'll be at the top in no time."

Then he smiled, turned around, and walked away. Squinting in the fierce sun, Angel and Victor watched him leave.

"These *menso* tourists," Angel said.

"Look," Victor said, seeing his chance. "I'm gonna go check it out. I'll call out if I find it."

Angel looked down at the snow and the drop without saying anything. He shook his head as Victor headed off in the direction of the hiker.

"Yeah, okay," he said. "Might as well check it out, if it's faster and all."

Victor exhaled deeply as he heard Angel walking behind him.

The boys backtracked about a quarter of a mile, following the man at a distance to where the trail veered upwards. They both realized instantly that here was the real trail. The pebbly path, easy to see all the way up the ridge, led right up through the jagged granite.

"We gotta say *thanks*," Victor said, breathing hard on the climb up.

"Hey, don't you think it's strange that he wasn't carrying a pack or anything like that?" Angel said.

"Yeah, not even water," Victor said. "Man, I'd be thirsty."

"Maybe his people are at the top and they have his stuff."

The stranger was already far ahead of them. He soon disappeared from view.

"We'll find him up there. No place else to go!" Victor said.

The rest of the hike was easy. *Pan comido*, Victor's mom would have said. Soon the two boys threw up their arms on the top of Mt. Tallac in celebration as if they had conquered Everest.

"Wow, this is awesome!" Victor said.

"*A toda madre!*" Angel agreed, meeting his friend's fist with his own.

Far below they saw Gilmore and Fallen Leaf lakes, where they often fished. Victor pointed out Lake Aloha, which had some spectacular spots for swimming. And, of course, they saw deep, blue, giant Lake Tahoe.

But what they didn't see was the stranger. Somehow he wasn't at the top.

"Weird, man," Victor said. "Where would he go? It's like he just vanished."

"Yeah," Angel said. "Weirder than your mom's tamales."

The boys sat in the dirt with their backs up against a rock and ate lunch. Angel took a long swig of warm soda and scared off a chipmunk with a thunderous burp.

"I'm gonna name him *Victor*," he said and laughed. "Cuz he's so brave."

Victor laughed too. Angel could make fun if he wanted.

The Killers

The bear appeared on the far shore. It stood there, untroubled by the pouring rain, eating from a shrub at the river's edge. Daniel and his dad didn't say a word. They just watched in awe.

They had seen so much on this trip. Northern lights that would have made his science teacher drool. *The dance of the spirits* is what the Cree called it. Astronomers couldn't explain it any better, Daniel thought. The white wolf he saw one morning across the river while picking berries for the pancakes. It had stared at him for a long time. Dozens of bald eagles. And all those black bears . . .

They had not seen another human being in almost a week. And only a handful before that. In a few days they would make it back to their car. Daniel had moments when he daydreamed of civilization. A hot shower and a comfortable bed. TV. A chocolate shake. And then another. But most of the time he didn't think of the time going by or of anywhere else he'd rather be.

Mostly when he thought, he thought of where he was at that moment and how it was good to be there. But as the days went by, he did less and less thinking and more and more just *being*. He fit into this life and this place like the wooden canoe paddle fit into his hands.

His blistered hands had toughened up and his shoulders didn't ache like at the beginning of the journey. When his father had suggested the trip, he had to look on a map to see where the place with the strange name was located. Now he would never forget *Saskatchewan*. Drinking the super strong cowboy coffee in the morning. The smell of the pike as it sizzled in the brown butter on the rare occasions when their fishing actually resulted in fish. Burning his tongue on the gooey, half-baked, half-burned frying pan brownies. These things would stay with him.

And the bears would stay with him. Seeing them didn't get old. The first bear walking along a bluff above the river as they paddled by. Then the mother with her two cubs exploring a marsh. And the one that came up to their tent at dawn. Daniel could barely make out its silhouette in the dark. Normally he slept in, but on this morning he was up early for some reason. The bear's curiosity had proved no match for a few shouts of "Yaw!" from his dad.

Each encounter was filled with a kind of magic. Time stopped and all there was, was the bear. Everything else faded away.

Across the river the bear kept eating.

Suddenly a motor boat appeared. The roar of the rapids drowned out the noise of its engine. While one man steered the little skiff through the turbulent and rocky waters, the one near the bow stood and raised a rifle. He had the bear in his sights.

"Noooo!" Daniel shouted over the sound of the water. The bear moved and then a shot rang out. And another. The bear became a blur, disappearing into the thick, wet forest.

The boat made its way over to them.

"How-dee," the helmsman said. "What brings you this way?"

"On vacation," Daniel's dad said.

The rifleman nodded slowly, glaring at Daniel, the weapon still in his hands. The two men looked dirty. It was easy to look dirty out in the wilderness, but this was the kind of dirty that didn't wash off with soap, Daniel thought.

"Well, we'll get the next one, sonny," the shooter said, grinning at Daniel with white and perfect teeth. "Don't lose any sleep over dat."

They both gave another half-hearted farewell nod and the boat continued upriver. Daniel and his father stood there in the mud and rain watching it until it disappeared, not speaking.

"We better start hauling this stuff," his dad finally said after a while. "We have a couple more big rapids to portage around today."

While his dad lifted their green canoe over his head, Daniel shouldered the heavy backpack. He bent down to pick up the paddles. As they walked down the muddy trail, he replayed the incident in his mind. He worried about the next bear the hunters would meet.

He thought about hunting in general. He tried not to think of it as a black and white, right or wrong thing like a child would, like he would have a few years earlier. He knew meat didn't grow on trees. And while he was starting to like vegetables more than when he was a little kid, no way was he ready to become a vegetarian. He loved burgers far too much for that. He understood that someone had to kill the cows for those burgers. Someone had to kill the pigs to make the pepperoni for his pizzas. Someone had to kill the chickens for his mom's awesome *milanesas*.

He understood all this but it didn't change anything. It didn't make him want to stop eating meat and it didn't change the fact that he didn't like the killing. He didn't want to be the kind of person who said one thing and did another. But there it was.

And that's what bothered him most about hunting: the hypocrisy. Most hunters didn't hunt for the meat and it wasn't a sport like they wanted people to believe. The truth, the way Daniel saw it, was that most hunters hunted for the kill. Hunting was just an excuse to kill. Killing was the whole point. The rest of it was fairy tales and camouflage.

They reached the end of the short path and put down their gear.

"I'm glad you saved that bear back there," his dad said. "I was thinking the same thing but my mouth got all dry and constipated."

"It just seemed wrong," Daniel said, smiling at his father's choice of words.

His dad nodded and looked at the new stretch of river before them. They turned back and went after the rest of their belongings.

When they reached the beginning of the trail, Daniel looked at the spot where the bear had been. He threw another pack over his shoulder and picked up the blue, plastic tub containing their food and looked around to make sure they didn't forget anything.

***

In the morning Daniel poked his head out the tent. Two loons swam on the foggy lake. Frost covered the ground. But as he stumbled outside, something else caught his eye.

There, right in front of their tent, was a bird head. The severed head of a large bird, maybe a falcon. The sight of it sent a chill down Daniel's spine that had nothing to do with the low temperature.

There was the smallest chance a predator had left it as an offering the way his cat would sometimes bring mice and birds back home to show Daniel what a great hunter he was. But it was much more likely that it had been placed there by humans. Daniel thought of two in particular who fit the bill.

Nothing else seemed to be disturbed. All their gear was where they had left it. The canoe. The paddles. Everything was fine. This was just a message.

"Do you think it was those guys?" Daniel asked.

"I don't think so," his dad said, lighting the little gas stove in preparation for breakfast. "Last we saw them they were traveling in the opposite direction. I didn't hear their motor again."

Of course, Daniel knew that after a long day of paddling and portaging he could sleep through a volcanic eruption. And his dad wasn't far behind. The men could have easily slipped into their camp during the night without being heard.

He couldn't shake the creepy feeling all day that someone was watching them. Even after the fog burned away and the sun filled the sky and they packed up and continued downriver. He just couldn't shake it.

***

Daniel was at one end of a long portage that skirted around some Class III rapids on the Churchill River. His father was somewhere at the opposite end. It was going to be their last long one. Portages

34

were commonly measured in rods, one rod equaling 16 and a half feet–the length of an average canoe. In Canada they used meters. But Daniel had learned the hard way that distance, however measured, was just one factor when it came to assessing a portage. Steepness, mud, rocks, roots, fallen trees, difficulty in loading and unloading, and the bloodthirstiness of the bugs were other critical considerations that could turn a short portage into a nightmare and make a long one fairly painless.

On lengthy portages it was better to haul the gear in a few shorter legs rather than one long one. It was easier on the back and shoulders and the mind to carry that weight and set it down, resting on the way back for more. And then coming back with a new load and going a little farther with it before re-turning for the original supplies. This leapfrogging technique broke up a big job into smaller, easier pieces.

Ideally, though, it would be best to carry every-thing in one trip. But being out here for two weeks made that impossible. Fourteen days worth of food weighed a lot. And all the little things that didn't weigh so much by themselves, all those little things that they brought along just in case, in the end add-ed up to a lot. So every portage required two trips.

Daniel and his father usually walked together on short paths. But with all those bears around, they split up on longer ones to cut down on the time they spent away from their food. Having to fight a bear for your food would not be fun. Especially since by then he would look at it as *his* food. And having to rely solely on fishing and berry picking for survival would not be fun either.

Daniel's thoughts returned to hunting. If he was going to be honest, he had to admit he liked guns, watching old war movies like *The Deer Hunter* with his grandfather, and killing anything that moved across the video game screen. And he loved to play paintball. It was a sweet thrill to nail one of his friends with one of those paint-filled pellets and hear them yell and curse.

"Bang, bang, baby, you're dead!" Daniel would call out. "Rest in pieces!"

The gun felt good in his hands too. It felt natural and right the way that little plastic guitar felt in his hands when he was slashing away on one of those songs on *Rock Band*.

But these things were games. Shooting a living thing with real bullets took things to a whole other level. It wasn't even the same thing. Killing something was a completely different thing and being able to tell the difference between such things was . . .

Ping! Something suddenly whizzed by Daniel's ear and off a rock. Then the air cracked a second time and a little mud kicked up a foot away from his right boot. Zlurp!

In an instant, Daniel was down hugging the ground. His heart and lungs screamed inside his chest as another projectile shattered the bark of a nearby tree. The small part of his brain that still worked wasn't exactly sure what was happening. Except that someone was shooting. And they were sure as *shitake* mushrooms shooting at him.

Daniel couldn't tell where the shots were coming from or where a good place to hide would be. He wasn't sure if he could or should even try to move. There wasn't much he could do. The cold, chocolatety mud plastered his cheek and oozed into his ear and he waited. He waited helplessly for the next shot.

He waited. And waited. And waited. And the next shot . . . never came.

After what seemed like a very long time, Daniel got up slowly. Cold and stiff, he began walking and then running toward the other end of the trail.

He worried about his dad. Was he all right? Had they shot at him too? Fighting the panic that quickly began to set in, he told himself that *he*– Daniel–had been the target. And that because of the trail length and the dense forest and the loud water, chances were good his dad had not even heard the shots. Still, he hurried.

"There you are," his dad said turning around. "I was beginning to think a bear got you."

"Did you hear those shots?" Daniel asked, his voice sounding like that of a scared child. "They were shooting at me."

"What?" his father shouted. "Who was shooting at you?"

Daniel told him what happened. He had never seen his dad so angry. His face turned a deep, purplish red and the veins in his neck and forehead bulged like strands of rope. He cursed and cursed and cursed some more.

"Those bass-turds! Those bass-turds!" he kept yelling. "Those bass-turds!"

Daniel started thinking that maybe it had been a mistake to tell him, but after a while his dad began to calm down. At one point he came over and bear-hugged Daniel for a long time.

They walked back to get the rest of their things. Everything was quiet, like it had never happened.

Later, while they loaded the canoe, his father talked about how they had to be careful the rest of the way. Careful not to be spotted by the men first. His dad's anger and outrage, no matter how strong, was no match for a loaded gun. They had to be smart. They would study the maps to see if they could find another route back to the car, a route that would cut down their time on the river. He talked about how they had to stay together. How those shooters were probably just trying to scare Daniel and teach him some sort of twisted lesson. How the police would probably not be able to do much since there was no real proof the bear hunters were the ones who had done the shooting. How none of it would matter when they got back.

They were still about 25 miles from the car. So far they had averaged 10-15 miles a day on the trip. But Daniel's dad decided they should *put the ash to 'er*, like the old timers used to say. He didn't want them to spend another night out here.

By mid-afternoon they reached Nipew Lake. The lake took its name, meaning *dead* in Cree, from a smallpox epidemic that swept through the area in the late 1700s. The wind had picked up like it usually did at that time of day. Small whitecaps already blanketed the water. On a normal day these were the types of conditions that would cause his dad to start looking for a campsite or at least a place to wait it out.

"It's blowing against us," his dad said. "But it's nothing we haven't done before."

They both knew that if the wind got strong enough, it could transform a big lake like this into a raging cauldron. An open canoe would have no chance. They would swamp for sure.

His dad always made Daniel wear his life vest. This time he did too. They secured their gear in the canoe with extra bungee cords and shoved off.

It was always safer to hug the shore when out on a large body of water. The old saying was you

39

shouldn't canoe anywhere you wouldn't want to be swimming. But since the shortest distance between two points is a straight line, they paddled down the middle of the lake, sometimes finding themselves almost a mile from the nearest shore.

As the wind blew harder, the waves grew larger. Daniel took off his old Hemingway-style fishing cap and shoved it inside his vest. At first they sang to help keep in rhythm. But at some point the singing died and they got quiet and just paddled as hard as they could.

Normally Daniel paddled on the same side until he got tired and then he would call out "switch" before paddling on the other side.

He could always tell when someone didn't know anything about canoeing when he saw them switching sides every few strokes. That's the only way rookies knew to keep the canoe going straight. What they didn't know was that all you needed for that was the *J*-stroke. You could keep the canoe straight by paddling on the same side and finishing each stroke with a little corrective curl.

But the wind was so strong that Daniel didn't dare switch sides even though his left arm ached something awful. The wind could easily rip the paddle out of his hands during such a maneuver. And they were really fighting to keep the canoe facing the waves now. If they eased up for a moment and got turned sideways, they would swamp for sure.

Daniel endured the pain and just kept cutting the blade of his paddle through the whipped-up water as the canoe rose and fell through the swells.

Larger and larger waves washed over the bow with increasing frequency, the cold water taking Daniel's breath away. The wind blew harder and the canoe–heavy from the water it was taking on–rode lower and lower in the growing waves.

It seemed impossible that they could hold on much longer.

Yet somehow they did. They paddled like this for almost an hour. Finally, the trees and rock shelves on the far shore began to get more defined. Closer. A little closer with every stroke. Relief washed over them and they began to talk again.

"We just might make it," his dad said. "If you don't sink us with the weight of all your pee."

"Have some," Daniel shouted back as he cupped a handful of water from the bottom of the canoe, flipping it over his shoulder.

By the time the canoe scraped across the gravelly beach, Daniel's butt was numb. He stumbled through the shallow water and held the canoe while his father got out.

"Good work!" his dad said, holding out a hand for Daniel to slap.

It was funny how the wind didn't seem to be that strong on land, the trees swaying gently. But back out behind them on the lake, the water was churning away like a blender. It didn't matter now. A few more short portages and a few more miles on the river and they would be back at the car.

***

The sun had gone down by the time they made it to their Jeep. The little parking lot was dark and quiet. No matter how good a trip had been, it was always good to see the car again. It meant you had made it. You had survived. This time that feeling was intensified several times over. His dad put his palm over the hood and bowed his head. Daniel just smiled.

He loaded the gear into the back of the SUV while his father strapped the canoe to the roof. The car rocked as he pulled hard on the lines. They were soon on the dirt road that would take them to the paved road that would take them to civilization.

Daniel sat there sore and drained of all energy but completely happy. It was the kind of mindless happiness that only comes after working to the point where the brain is mostly not there anymore and all it understands is that the work is over.

Images of the trip came back to him and he was filled with the whole of it. Not just the shooting. He would remember the trip for everything it was. And so much of it had been good. Better than good.

"I remember seeing a motel up a ways when we came in," his dad said, tapping his fingers on the steering wheel. "I think there's a restaurant nearby too. I'm guessing they'll probably be able to whip you up a chocolate sh . . ."

Suddenly there was a loud exploding pop and the car jerked to the left. Daniel jumped. His father pulled the car off to the side of the road.

"That was kind of scary, huh?" he said, sighing deeply. "I think we've got a flat. One more little portage to get through."

They got out to look at the damage. It was moonless and hard to see, no end of stars filling the cold sky. Summer still had a month or so to go on the calendar but it was over in this part of the world. It was going to be sweet to sleep in a warm bed tonight, Daniel thought.

As they got busy digging in the back for a flashlight and the spare and the jack, a car pulled up behind them. It had its lights off.

Two men got out.

Has Anybody Here Seen Hank?

Five little words put a stake through the heart of what was going to be the best summer of Steve's life.

"Time for a job, son," his stepdad said one night in early June. "You're not a kid anymore and it's time to learn the value of hard work."

Steve hated when Hank called him son. He was not his son. He had never known his real father, but a lot would have to change before he thought of Hank that way. He had only been married to his mom for two years and that wasn't nearly enough time.

But Steve wasn't thinking about Hank's use of the word *son* now. He was too focused trying to make some sense of those terrible letters scraping and scratching at the inside of his brain: J-O-B. They rolled around in there like skateboarders in an empty swimming pool.

"A job?" he repeated.

"You'll thank me some day, I promise," Hank said.

His dream of driving around town all summer with his buddies cruising for girls and spending days lost in his favorite video game was dying faster than a vampire left out in the midday sun. Hank got up from the sofa and took his large frame to the kitchen.

"Loser," Steve mumbled under his breath. "Total loser. What was she *thinking*?"

By mid-July it had become his life. If it could be called a life. Steve's days were swallowed up whole as he sweated and dumped pieces of skin, bone, and cartilage into large silver vats of boiling oil at *Harry's Chicken*.

Dealing with the customers was even worse. The place was packed with Hanks. Losers, one and all. Eight hours a day of this left Steve feeling as dead as those birds and in one foul mood. The clock was broken, he was sure of it, but somehow the summer was flying by on wet chicken wings.

One hot night in August, Steve assumed his usual spot on the sofa and stared through the TV, smelling of old grease and ripe armpits. Hank came in and sunk down into the recliner.

"How was work today, son?" he asked.

"Fine," Steve slurred, never taking his eyes off the screen.

"You know, I was thinking," Hank said. "You and me should do something fun this weekend. Just the two of us. We've both been working real hard this summer and we deserve some fun."

"Sorry, no can do," Steve said. "Have plans to go skateboarding with Todd."

He didn't have any such plans. But he was still mad at Hank. And if it didn't consume so much energy–energy he didn't have–he probably would have hated him. There was no freakin' way he was going to waste his weekend having "some fun" with Hank.

There was a long silence.

"That's all right," Hank said. "We'll do it another time."

More silence followed and then Steve heard someone say, "Nah, I guess Todd and I can always go boarding another time . . . "

There must be some other loser in the room, Steve thought. Who's Hank talking to? Well, whatever, it was awful big of him to throw himself on that grenade. *I owe you one, buddy.*

And then it hit Steve like an 18-wheeler plowing through his head. *He* had said those words. He had said those words and he knew he had to quit that job before it ate the rest of his brain. He must have mad chicken disease for sure. Steve just kept staring off past *Wheel of Fortune*, unable to buy a vowel–or a clue.

His stepdad woke him up early on Saturday morning.

"Guess what we're doing?" Hank said, like some child talking about the presents *Santy Claus* would bring him.

"I don't know, you tell me," Steve said, rubbing his crusty, sleep-filled eyes and wondering why it was still dark outside.

"Well, I'll tell you since you'll never guess anyways," Hank said. "We're going rafting today, sport! Isn't that great?"

Steve had never been rafting before. In fact, he had only been on a boat of any kind once in his life and that had not gone well. He ended up barfing his breakfast and then yellow bile over the side of *The Star Rover* into the choppy Pacific Ocean. His prayers for a quick death went unanswered. Or maybe the answer was, "Just keep tossing them cookies, boy." He swam away from the memory and faked a smile.

"Great," he said without emotion.

The ride down to the river was dusty and bumpy. The shuttle bus smelled of sunscreen and mildew and overheated plastic and was full of excited tourists dressed in baseball caps and plaid shorts and river sandals. It was loud, with mindless clucking punctuated by occasional fits of cackling. Steve and Hank were quiet the entire way.

When the bus eventually came to a squeaky stop, everyone filed out one by one. Steve saw the river for the first time. It looked peaceful and harmless as it made its way around the bend. He let out a sigh. This was not the ocean. He might even be able to catch up on a little sleep as they floated down stream.

"All righty, folks, if I could have y'all gather round here for a moment," said a shirtless man with a thick, red beard. "My name's Jedediah and before we get started, I'm gonna teach y'all some things that might help you survive your little trip down this here river."

As the man talked about safety and the dangers of the river, everyone got quiet. Steve thought that he probably played it up to make the tourists feel like they were getting their money's worth.

"This is just going to be the best!" Hank said as they got into the raft.

There was a sudden lurch as one of the plaid tourists stepped inside the boat and lost his balance on top of the swaying, rubber floor. He landed hard on the seat, missing Hank by just a few inches.

These were the types of people who ate that chicken, Steve thought, starting to get angry. He tried to focus on the water and the trees and the fact that he would still be able to get back to town by the afternoon and do something with his friends.

They pushed off from shore and began drifting downriver behind the other four rafts in their group. There were seven people in their raft, three on each side plus the guide—who ended up being the same red-bearded man giving the opening speech. And he was still talking in that fake Disney Country Bear Jamboree drawl.

"If you've got nerves now, don't worry cuz you'll be happier than flies on diarrhea after we get through 'em rapids!" he said.

The sun danced on the water and there were fields of black, shiny obsidian rocks on each side of the river. Steve didn't know all this beauty existed so near his everyday life.

He soon began hearing the faint sound of fast water in the distance. It started out like a whisper, but became louder and louder with each stroke of his blue and red plastic paddle.

"First one's coming up!" the guide yelled. "Remember, just do what I say and everything will be just fine."

And it was. The first set of rapids weren't really so bad at all. Steve was amazed to find that he was smiling and even laughing as the boat heaved up and down in the waves. And his stomach was fine.

"Oh, man, that was awesome!" he said.

Hank grinned at him and everyone else in the boat was smiling with a mix of relief and excitement.

"Yeah, that one's always a blast," said the guide. "It's this next one you gotta worry about."

Steve was suddenly happy, something he hadn't felt in a long time, and was looking forward to what was to come. He tuned out *Ol' Country Bear* and paddled and thought about how Hank was right. This was fun.

The quiet section went on for a while, but then the air was filled again with the roar of crashing water. The other rafts were far ahead, making it seem like they were the only ones on the river. The guide wiped his forehead with the back of his hand.

The river started to get rough and the boat bounced up and down, slapping at water and air. There was no turning back now.

"Paddle!" the guide shouted above the roar.

Steve began to dig his paddle into the water, but it was difficult to develop a rhythm in the growing waves. And then the river began to turn mean. A huge splash of water shot across the front of the boat, soaking everyone. Steve gasped in shock. It was freezing! For a moment he stopped paddling. The current pushed the boat sideways into another huge wave.

"Paddle!" *Country Bear* shouted again from the back of the spinning boat, which was now the front and now the back again. Steve began moving his arms in a paddling motion, but all he seemed to be hitting was air. The boat slammed hard against a boulder.

And then it happened.

It happened in slow motion and with the sound turned off. In real time it only took a few seconds. But in Steve's mind time slowed down and he could see Hank's paddle fly through the air and Hank slide off the red rubber raft, the soles of his cheap river sandals the last to go. Their eyes met at some point. And then he was gone.

"Hank!" Steve yelled as everything sped up again and the volume turned up to 11.

The boat spun violently away from the boulder. Steve searched the thrashing water for any sign. He yelled again. The guide was yelling too and jerking his head from side to side looking for Hank while still trying to maintain some control of the boat.

Steve thought about the many times he had wished for something like this to happen. For Hank to be gone and out of his life. But now, as he frantically scanned the raging waves, fear and sorrow welled up in Steve's throat as he realized he was losing another father–the only real father he had ever known.

He spotted the red baseball cap bobbing in between waves. Hank's big dumb red Angels cap. But where was Hank? There was no sign of him. What if his foot was stuck under a rock and he was drowning? What would Steve tell his mom?

The clock in his mind broke again and the seconds felt like minutes and three minutes is all you get, he thought. Three minutes without oxygen and that's it. *C'mon, Hank, c'mon! Where are yooou!*

"Look, there he is!" the man sitting behind him suddenly said, gripping Steve's shoulder.

Hank was floating on his back in the middle of the river, his head bobbing in and out of view. Steve couldn't tell if he was hurt or even conscious.

"We've got to get over there!" Steve screamed.

Country Bear made a sweeping motion with his paddle and steered the boat toward the middle of the river. Steve paddled with all his might. His muscles burned with the effort.

Hank's face looked livid and very small now. Steve threw his paddle inside the raft as they got close to him and leaned over the side of the boat. But all he managed to do was scratch at Hank's lifejacket as he went by. The boat spun around, leaving Hank out of reach again.

Then a huge wave lifted him up and brought Hank close to the raft. One of the tourists at the back lunged and grabbed onto Hank's lifejacket. Steve could only watch as Hank's face disappeared under the turbulent water. Then the man readjusted his grip and dug his feet deep in the boat and pulled Hank's body up and over the side. The man and Hank landed with a hard, wet bounce onto the floor of the raft.

"Hank! Hank! Are you all right?" Steve yelled, grabbing his arm.

He noticed that both of Hank's knees were bleeding. He was shaking and looked gray around the eyes. But then Steve saw his chattering teeth break into a smile.

"Jeez, that was crazy out th-th-there, son," Hank said. "But I think I'm okay, just a few scrapes."

As the raft entered another stretch of calm water, Steve sighed and thought about how it could have turned out. How it almost did turn out. They had been lucky. Steve looked at the man who had pulled his stepfather to safety. He was surprised to see that it was the clumsy guy who had almost crashed into Hank at the beginning of the trip. He was soaked and his sunglasses were missing one of the lenses and he was still breathing hard.

"Thank you, sir," Steve said, sticking out his hand. He hoped that the man could somehow read past the empty, cliché gesture and get a little sense of the deep gratitude Steve was feeling.

The man shook his hand, giving him a little *ain't-no-big-thing* nod. The other people in the boat were quiet. Even *Country Bear*. The warm sun shone down and began to dry out the wet things.

"I thought I had lost you, *Da* . . . Hank," Steve suddenly blurted out when they were back on the shuttle bus. "You shouldn't go scaring people like that."

Hank just nodded and smiled. Steve knew he was grinning at what had almost slipped out of his mouth. He turned away toward the window and smiled too.

The Music
of Falling Down

Thwuck!

Something crashed into the living room window. Jessica had been drinking coffee in the kitchen, watching the sun paint the winter dawn shades of orange and red not found in any box of pastels, and trying to wake up.

She put her mug down and walked over to the window. The bird had been lucky, losing only a few feathers before flying off in a better direction. Since they had moved into this house of glass and trees, Jessica had become an expert of sorts on bird brain injuries. It seemed glass was not programmed into their DNA, so the birds just thought they could fly in one window and out the other. Their injuries ranged from glancing blows to collisions that killed them outright, long before they hit the ground.

She had nursed some back to health and watched others never leave the shoebox hospital she placed them in. The neighbor's cat slashed at her with its eyes, green and hate-filled, when she beat him to the scene of an accident.

"Be more careful next time," she said to the tiny feathers lying on the front porch.

Jessica finished her coffee and focused on the run ahead. An easy 10. She smiled and thought about how running 10 miles could actually feel easy at times, but leaving a warm bed at 5:57 in the morning never did. She questioned her sanity and stretched and yawned and told herself it was worth it.

"This is what it takes," she thought. "Somewhere out there someone else is training."

She got dressed, put her shoes on, grabbed her key, and picked up her MP3 player. She shuffled through the playlists, searching for that extra ounce of inspiration. A lot of tunes sound good early in a run, but it took a special song to hold up toward the end of one.

She went back to the bathroom and got a fistful of toilet paper. Winter running made her nose run as much as her legs sometimes. Reaching the front door, she looked down at the shoe studs she wore to give her better traction during icy conditions. Not today, she thought. The fresh snow covering the world outside wouldn't turn to ice for several days. As long as it wasn't too deep, new snow provided good footing and was fun to run on. She locked the door behind her and pocketed the house key.

Kathleen Edwards sang *Goodnight, California* as Jessica jogged easily down the street. She was glad to have recently discovered the Canadian songwriter. The songs were gritty and beautiful at the same time.

Squirrel tracks peppered the soft mashed-potato snow. It was quiet and cold and the sun had disappeared behind light gray clouds. Jessica didn't need a weatherman to tell her more snow was on the way.

She felt the life slowly returning to her body. Taking in the beauty that surrounded her, she increased her speed to match the growing intensity of the songs. It was a good playlist. And it was a good day to run.

She turned off the deserted street and took a trail into the woods. She would make a loop of it, dropping down to the river, staying by the water for a few miles before cutting back up. She liked this route because it pushed her when she needed it the most: on the last half. It was uphill all the way back home.

She was really starting to feel it by the time Kirk Hammett began thrashing away on *One*. It was a song her older brother had turned her on to. Not perfect to run to as a whole–the lyrics were super depressing and the tempo dragged at times–but when it started to rock, it was epic.

"Wait for me!" Jessica shouted as the screaming guitars and drums dragged her down the trail.

She thought about the upcoming track season and how she had some speed in her but her real strength was distance. The longer the race, the more time there was to wear down the competition. The coach said Jessica had the right mental toughness for the long events. She thought about the speech she had to give in her English class next week. She thought about how maybe this time she might be able to get through it without her voice getting all high and shaky. *Maybe.*

She thought about everything and nothing. And she ran.

Suddenly a grayish-brown dog appeared on the trail 100 feet ahead. Pausing the music, she slowed and then stopped. The dog watched her for a moment before running off up a steep embankment. Jessica smiled when it dawned on her that it had been a wolf. When she passed the spot where it had crossed the trail, she looked up and saw it again. The animal studied her with hypnotic, yellow eyes. After a time the wolf left, leaving Jessica filled with wonder and gratitude for living in such a place. Some people didn't like Idaho. She was not one of them.

She continued down the trail.

Though her music player was still turned off, a Journey song started playing in her head. She changed the lyrics to "Someday *wolves* will find you" while she accompanied herself on air organ like the keyboard player in the convulsively goofy video.

Jessica laughed, thinking how dumb she could be sometimes and how sometimes there was nothing better than a good laugh at your own expense.

Soon the trail dropped down steeply into a shady area where the sun rarely hit. The air was colder down here. She looked at her watch and thought about the time. She was a little off pace.

"Pick it up," she told herself. "Pick it up."

As Jessica sped up, her shoe suddenly cut through a thin layer of snow, hitting an old patch of glass-smooth ice below. One foot and then the other failed to grip the ground and Jessica lost her balance. It all seemed to happen in a kind of hopeless and helpless slow motion and lightning fast at the same time. Her legs flew up in front of her. Her upper back hit the ice first, her head bouncing hard off the thick, solid, silver surface a moment later.

Finding it hard to breathe, she felt an intense pain in her head and then the stars came out and the darkness closed in all around. Blackness and nothingness swallowed her.

Jessica slowly came to at some point. She had a killer headache. Her brain felt like it had been in a cage fight. *And lost*. She didn't know how long she had been out. She was cold, so she knew it had been a while. Steam rose from a small pool of blood in front of her face. She touched her head and found that the blood was coming from her right ear.

Not good, she thought.

"Not good," she whispered.

The sight of blood always left her queasy, but she was not afraid now. Felt no emotion. A thick fog fell over her feelings and if some part of her was scared, she was utterly disconnected from that part.

She thought of the wolf. Would he return and bring friends? She knew there were coyotes and mountain lions in these woods too. The blood was an invitation to them all.

She tried to stand, head pounding, dizzy. Spinning, everything spinning. A sea of nausea washed over her stomach. She stumbled and sat back down.

She sat and stared. At nothing. Stared out far into the distance. Beyond the endless, white distance. There, but not really there.

It had started to snow. *Can't stay here.* Waiting for someone to come for help was not an option. *Try it again. Get up. Slowly this time.*

Jessica stood and the world of white spun around her again and she closed her eyes and bent over, hands on knees. She stayed like that for a long time and the spinning eased. She opened her eyes and saw the snowflakes melting as they hit the dark red pool.

She took a few wobbly steps back up the trail, stepping cautiously by the spot that had taken her down. The back of her left knee didn't feel right.

And neither did her head, the pain now replaced by a strange numbness. But she kept moving. Mostly she walked slowly, but sped up as best she could when she started feeling cold.

It was going to be a long walk home.

Many times she stumbled and many times she thought of sitting down. But she didn't. Just kept putting one foot in front of the other. *Keep moving. Keep moving. Keep moving.*

By the time Jessica made it back to her still sleepy street, the bleeding had stopped. Her hair was matted down. Like dry mud cracking on skin, the brown blood caked to the side of her face began to hurt. Must be quite the sight, she thought. Stepping on the porch, she noticed the little feathers were all gone. She nodded.

"What happened to you?" her dad asked with concern in his voice when she walked in.

Jessica started to say she was okay but then a scythe-sharp pain split her skull and she reached out a trembling hand to hold herself up. The blackness came back and she fell again. The distance to the ground was not that far. Strange how Jessica felt herself falling much farther.

***

Her running shoes are under the hospital bed. The machines beep and hum and the pumps pump and the nurses come and go. The doctor tells her parents she does not know when–or if–Jessica will wake up from the coma. Tears run down their pale cheeks. They will have to wait, the doctor says. Just wait.

But somewhere behind the closed eyes, in the shadowy, sinuous canyons of her sleep-mind, Jessica isn't waiting. She is running. The snow is falling gently, her shoes crunching the white carpet that covers everything. She runs fast and free, not waiting for her body to follow, not waiting for her mind to find her. No time to lose if she's going to catch up to that wolf. *Where we goin' for breakfast?*

She runs hard and easy and on and on and on and she does not slip, does not fall. She just keeps running into the distance. The endless, white distance.

Forward Progress

The freshly starched collar felt like a noose as Matt sat with his parents and little sister in church. He knew he should try to focus on what the preacher was saying. But it was early and he had other things on his mind.

He turned and nodded sleepily at Mason who was sitting with his family three rows behind him.

Later, at the crowded diner, Matt played with his half-raw hash browns. His mom talked about getting the house ready for Thanksgiving. Pouring more hot sauce on his scrambled eggs, his dad nodded.

"That man's Sunday is burnt toast," Matt thought, feeling sorry for his dad. "She's gonna have him doing so many chores, he'll be lucky if he can catch two plays in a row."

Matt had something more fun in mind for his day than working around the house or watching the Seahawks lose another game.

When they got home, he ran upstairs, tore off his shirt and tie, and put on his favorite old sweatshirt.

After lacing up his hiking boots, he checked the flashlight and spare batteries.

"Later!" he said, going out the door.

Mason was waiting for him across the street on his porch. They met in the middle of the road.

"Ready, Freddie?"

"Ready, Eddie. And don't call me Freddie."

"Roger that."

"And don't call me Roger either."

"Shirley."

Their legs moved quickly over the trail of dead, soggy leaves. It was hard going uphill, but not as hard as the year had been so far.

Matt's mom had insisted on a private middle school even though they could barely afford it. Being at a new school—far from his friends—was rough. Here it was mid-November and he was still struggling with the transition.

Another dusting of snow covered more and more of the ground as they gained elevation. It was only a matter of time before the snow came in earnest. But not today. Today was crisp and clear.

They were headed for Little Smith Cave. It didn't have a cool name like *Dead Man's Cave* or *Satan's Fun Pit*, but it was theirs. The fact that it was four uphill miles from town helped to keep away the dubious partiers that frequented the caves closer to civilization. And the fact that the tunnel system was fairly short and straightforward kept away the serious spelunkers. They had been here dozens of times over the years and seen only a handful of people.

The cave had taken on special significance for Matt lately. It was good to have something constant in his life. The cave was always 42 degrees. If it was summer. If it was winter. If he was 9. If he was 12. If his mom was mad at him. If he had to go to a stupid, uptight new school. The cave was always 42 degrees. And Mason was always with him.

They took out their flashlights as they began to descend the short side trail to the mouth of the lava tube.

"Well, she told me she misses you!" Mason said several minutes after they had entered the cave.

Matt drove his fist hard into his friend's upper arm, sending the flashlight crashing off the cave wall. The light went out.

"What, man? Don't do harm to the messenger," Mason said, rubbing his arm and bending over to pick up his light. "I was just supposed to relay that to you. I mean, I miss you over there too."

Matt listened to Mason's voice as it bounced off the walls and ceiling before disappearing into the sandy floor. During rare quiet moments, he could hear the water dripping off the icy stalactites over-head. Here with his friend, in these familiar sur-roundings, sometimes it almost felt as if nothing had changed.

Mason kept playing with his flashlight, but it wouldn't come back on.

"You've gone and busted it, you *fool*," he said.

They were down to one light source now. But we have plenty of spare batteries, Matt thought. No worries.

"I got your back," he said. "Hang tight."

Two hours later they reached the end of the cave. They had to crawl the last section where the ceiling hung low. They sat in the sand with their backs to the cool rock wall without speaking. Matt wondered what it must have been like to be a caveman. He thought about Katie missing him.

"All right," Mason said after a while. "I hunger for pizza. Let's start back and you can treat, preppie."

Pizza did sound good, Matt thought. Plus he had homework to do. Homework on a Sunday night! Man, that sucked. He was pretty sure cavemen didn't have any homework.

"You're on, brocephus," he said.

They began heading back.

"And there we were sitting in class," Mason was saying, "and he just spewed all over the back of her head! I mean, all …"

Suddenly the flashlight went out.

"Stop your clownin'!" Mason said.

Matt first checked the on-off switch and then began shaking and tapping the flashlight. It had gone out suddenly, not gradually like when the batteries start to go. Just out. Like when a bulb burns out.

They were in total darkness. Thick and deep and claustrophobic.

"I'm not playing, man," Matt said. "I think it's dead."

"Let me see," Mason said, reaching out blindly. "Let's try changing the batteries."

They fumbled with the batteries for several minutes, repositioning them every possible way. It was useless.

"We'll just stick close to the wall," Matt said. "It's gonna be slow but we'll make it."

Mason didn't answer. Matt felt a twinge of fear deep in his stomach.

At some point, Matt remembered his watch had a night light. Each green glow lasted about three seconds. It didn't provide much light, but it gave them a little relief from the black-on-black monotony.

After a while Matt decided that it wasn't so bad. Progress was slow because of all the rocks and uneven footing, but they were moving steadily toward their goal. Mason had even started talking again. And had not stopped. All right by me, Matt thought. The chatter kept his mind from focusing on the dark and the doubts that came with it.

They knew this cave. They knew there was one way in and one way out. And they would soon be out.

But something hard had slowly taken hold inside Matt. Something that pushed aside the fear he had felt when the light had first gone out. Before Matt was sure what was happening, he was overcome with a sick feeling. Suddenly he started shouting.

"I can't stand it anymore! I hate that school! I hate my mom for making me go! I hate the uniforms! I hate the rules and the teachers and . . . "

He dropped to his knees, beating the sand with his fists in the dark. His hands were cold and filled with rage. He felt his face get hot and his eyes burn. And for the first time since the lights went out, he was glad it was dark.

Not knowing what to say, Mason was quiet.

"Sorry, man," Matt said later in a nasally voice. "Didn't mean to have a meltdown in my diaper."

"I was wondering what that smell was," Mason said. "We're good—as long as you don't expect me to change you."

***

They sat in silence, feeling foolish and frustrated.

More than an hour after the darkness had closed in, they reached the end of the cave. They had been stumbling along for what seemed like forever. And now they were back. Back to the end of the cave where the ceiling came down low. In the dark, they had gone the wrong way!

"At least now we know what direction we have to go," Mason sighed. "Let's do it."

"Deal," Matt answered as *4:23* glowed up at him from his watch.

They shuffled slowly, numb fingers sliding across the smooth cave wall.

It was time to face what was going on. They would make it out of the cave. It would be dark when they got above ground. But they would eventually get home, maybe even before the second half of Sunday Night Football.

Darkness was not the problem. Kids are afraid of the dark, Matt thought, but it's what's there in the light that's scarier sometimes.

No matter how much he wanted things to stay the same, things were changing. So much had already changed and there would be more changes to come. And as much as he wanted, Matt couldn't stop it. There was no going back.

There was nothing else to do but move forward.

Water Under the Bridge

They pulled off the river and walked down to where they could see the rapids below. The stretch was full of large rocks and snags and they quickly spotted the canoe in the middle of the angry water.

"There they are," her dad said, rubbing the black stubble on his chin.

Ali and her dad had been in the vast, lonely Canadian wilderness for over a week now and the red canoe was the first they had seen since they had launched. It had been ahead of them as they crossed the large lake.

Suddenly the canoe banged up hard against a rock, spun around, and capsized.

"Oh, no," Ali said.

The two men and their gear flew into the turbulent water. It was a horrible sight. Ali and her dad ran down shore, but the men were far from them now, in the middle of the river, their bodies like rag dolls, thrown mercilessly in the steady pound of churning water.

There was nothing to do but watch. And hope.

After a moment, they could see two heads downriver.

"Look, they're okay," her dad said. "They're through the worst part. They just need to hang on. See them?"

"Yeah."

"Okay," he said. "I guess it's our turn."

Ali's stomach gave definite signs that her breakfast wanted to run screaming out the nearest exit. She knew they had to get through these rapids, but the thought made her sweaty and cold at the same time. They made a study of the river, and saw that they needed to stay on the right side to avoid the largest waves. They walked back to their green Old Town Penobscot and clipped on their orange life vests.

"Ready?" her dad yelled over the rushing water.

"Ready!"

They paddled hard into the rapids. The river turned choppy. They angled to the right, her dad shouting directions about which side she needed to paddle on. He steered them past submerged rocks and they shot right through with no problems.

"Yeah!" Ali shouted.

Her dad cheered too and as the water slowed down, they clicked their paddles together in celebration as they always did after a successful run. This was the seventh set of rapids on the trip so far.

They looked for the men and soon found them on shore, pulling gear from the water. The men waved and signaled that they were okay and didn't need anything. Ali and her dad paddled on into the gray morning.

"Capsizing is hard on the spirit," her dad said after a few minutes. "They seem all right, though. Could've been worse."

Ali and her dad had never been dumped into the water on any of their canoe trips, and there had been a lot over the years. But they also had never been down so much whitewater before. They were on the Churchill River, which wound through some of the most unspoiled and desolate wilderness in the world. The river pushed through large lakes and down rapids and was mostly untouched by civilization. It was the same route that the French Canadian voyageurs had used hundreds of years ago, paddling in long canoes and trading with the natives for beaver pelts and animal furs.

"What a life!" her dad had said as they drove from Oregon. "Even though it was hard going, the voyageurs were happy and free. They smoked pipes, sang songs as they crossed huge lakes, and ran dangerous rapids. They were out for months at a time, in all types of weather."

Her dad had wanted to do this canoe trip for years. She was relieved when he asked her to come along, especially since the separation.

"It'll be the trip of a lifetime!" he had said.

And it had been. She loved being out in the wilderness with her dad. But she was hoping for something more. Some words. An explanation. Maybe even a promise to come back. There were only a few more days left in the trip, and her dad remained as quiet as ever on the subject.

It was a stormy morning with steady rain dropping down from a series of dark and quick-moving clouds. The air was heavy from all the humidity.

The next rapids were too dangerous to run. They found the portage trail and unloaded their gear. While her dad hoisted the canoe up over his head, Ali carried the food pack, life vests, and paddles. They walked along the narrow, muddy trail that bypassed the rough waters and led them to a calmer section of the Churchill.

The rain was suffocating. Ali's blue raincoat and pants made her feel like a giant, soggy sponge. She was soaked on the outside from the rain and on the inside from sweat. After two trips back and forth, they sat on a small beach eating lunch before continuing downriver. As they ate, mosquitoes zeroed in, having their own lunch and adding to the many bites Ali already had.

"I wish it would clear up," she said, swatting away the bloodsuckers.

"Me too," her dad said.

Finally, by late afternoon, a streak of blue appeared in the sky.

They camped on a hill overlooking Sandy Lake, about a mile up from Snake Rapids. Ali was thankful they couldn't hear the roar, as she didn't want to sleep with rushing water echoing in her ears all night. For dinner, they ate frying pan cornbread along with beef stew from a can. They sat around the smoky campfire, watching the sky.

"You up for the Snake tomorrow?" her dad asked.

"Yeah, I think so," she said.

Snake Rapids would be the toughest of the trip, full of deadheads and hidden rocks, and one large, dark whirlpool. At one point, Ali started shivering uncontrollably just thinking about what those rapids would look like up close. The guidebook had mentioned that two people had drowned there a few years back.

"It's scary to think about it though," Ali said. "Especially after seeing those guys today."

"We'll do fine."

Her dad stood up. It had been a grueling, wet day. Even before the last of the light faded away, they headed to bed.

But it was a long, bad night. Ali stayed awake in her sleeping bag long after her dad drifted off into slumber and snores. She thought of big, black waves and empty canoes bouncing along furious rivers. She thought of bone-white rapids and dark whirlpools. She thought of heads without bodies in the waves. She thought of her dad and his frustrating silences and wondered why he didn't talk to her about why he had left. The real reason. She thought of the stack of cardboard boxes she had found in the garage before she knew and that sinking, awful feeling she felt coming home when she opened the front door and remembered that he wasn't there.

Turning cannibal, her thoughts devoured her brain. The more she tried not to think of all these things, the more she did think of these things. Finally, in the early hours of the morning, exhaustion engulfed her and she surrendered to sleep.

The day was blue with no wind. They paddled to the edge of the lake and could hear the menacing roar of Snake Rapids. As they approached, her dad said that there was a little problem: he couldn't see any shoreline to pull off and scout.

"That's a *huge* problem," Ali said. Her heart thundered inside her chest, vibrating throughout her body.

Wet mist floated toward them, hitting Ali in the face. The sound was getting louder as they glided over the water with no effort. She scanned the sides of the river and saw that her dad was right. No shoreline.

"Must be a high water year," he said. "Probably a snowy winter."

Ali turned and looked at her dad as the canoe continued to drift toward the inevitable. She could feel the tug of the current pulling at them. In the distance, a bridge extended over the river.

"We'll have to go to Plan B," her dad said. "We'll use the book."

He started reading out loud.

"Stay left until you cross under the bridge. There is a large whirlpool that needs to be avoided on river right. The waves begin in a minor way but build up to large, freestanding waves. After you cross under the bridge, go to the middle in the fast channel of water. Stay in the main channel of the river the rest of the way. This is one fast ride."

Ali put down her paddle, wiping her sweaty palms on her pants.

"I wish we could pull off to see," she said. Her voice was a pitch or so higher than usual and her mouth was dry as cornmeal. Eyes bulging, she took one last long drink from her water bottle.

The canoe began picking up speed as the lake washed into the raging Churchill River. The white-water roar got louder and Ali could see in the distance the foamy peaks of what they were heading toward. The bridge was in full view now.

"Ali, listen to me," her dad said. "We're going to do this. We're going to shoot through these rapids like pros."

She glanced back and tried to smile. The lake behind them looked so peaceful. She wanted to be there.

"Okay," she said, holding down her fear. "Okay, we can do this."

"Paddle hard," her dad said.

Ali pushed her paddle through the strong river. They stayed on river left, far from the whirlpool.

"Keep paddling!"

They shot past the bridge, scraping a huge boulder on the way by. The front of the canoe veered to the left and they started going into the waves sideways, but her dad straightened them out quickly. She looked ahead at the mammoth waves they were paddling into.

"Not there, Dad!" Ali shouted, pointing. "Not there!"

She thought that there was no way they would be able to ride over those humongous monsters. They floated over the first huge wave and Ali was thrown high up into the air, her butt landing back down hard on the cane seat. She was relieved she was still in the canoe. But then she saw that there were many more waves, all in a row, all bigger, and it felt as if they had no control anymore. She threw her paddle in and hung on to the gunwales.

"My *God*," she whispered into the roar of the rapids.

This was like nothing they had run before. A surge of water slammed into them. She rubbed her face, gasping for breath as another huge wave hit. Seconds later the canoe dropped down in the trough of the biggest wave yet. Looking up, Ali shuddered at the huge, black wall of water coming right toward them.

"Dad!" she screamed.

The water smashed into her, knocking her backwards. A sharp pain pierced her shoulder as the canoe swayed violently to the left, barely missing a group of jagged rocks and almost tipping.

"Lean to the right," her dad yelled. "Right, Ali! Now!"

She leaned over and the canoe balanced out. She tried to say something, but the saliva in her mouth had evaporated and the words got stuck in her throat.

They rode over each of the large waves, one at a time, their tiny canoe bouncing and jerking in the river. At the top of each wave, Ali shut her eyes tightly before the fast drop down, each time half expecting a cold plunge into the water. But they stayed afloat.

Ali grabbed her paddle when she noticed that the waves were getting smaller. She turned to catch a glimpse of her dad. He was serious and focused.

Ali knew that those deep lines in his face would remain until they were past the rapids. But looking at him, she now realized that they would be okay, that calmer waters were just ahead.

Grin and Bear It

A deep line formed between Emily's eyes as she squinted down at a pile of bear scat while her dad explained how a lot could be learned by studying an animal's fecal matter.

"Look there," he poked and pointed with a branch. "You see what's left of those pine nuts?"

A lot of 12-year-old girls might be a little put off by the subject matter, but Emily wasn't like most girls her age. She enjoyed her dad's bathroom humor as much as any boy would. Plus, she loved learning things.

Suddenly Emily heard a terrible growl. She spun around and saw a huge brown bear running down the trail toward her. Her dad had disappeared and the forest was purple, cold, and dark. Somehow, though, she could see the bear perfectly. Its glowing, crazed eyes closed in, no more than 20 feet away now.

A split second later, as the grizzly towered over her, Emily raised her arms over her head. The bear let fly a deafening roar. It was so close she could smell its awful, rotting fish breath as it swung its head from side to side, drool dangling from its mouth.

The claws came toward her like lightning. Too fast for Emily to run or even duck. She felt them rip into the side of her face as she flew through the air from the force of the blow. Everything turned warm and red. The bear closed in again. Coming closer. Closer . . .

"Ahhh!" Emily woke with a scream, sweat on her upper lip. "Oh, man."

It seemed so real, she thought, trying to catch her breath. She raised her head off the damp, lumpy pillow and saw a dark shape next to her on the bed. It was the book she had been reading when she fell asleep: *Dead and Bear-ied*, a gruesomely-detailed collection about people who had been killed by bears.

"Genius move," Emily sighed, pushing the book away. "Get back to sleep now."

She counted backwards from 100 and, after several restarts, at some point passed out. She awoke in the morning to the smell of coffee and bacon, the sun coming in low through a crack in the curtain.

After breakfast they were back exploring the national park. Her dad and younger sister, Danielle, led the way while Emily–recovering from her psychic mauling and still feeling more zombie than human–brought up the rear. The short trail they were on hugged the rim hundreds of feet above the Yellowstone River. Emily was hoping to see some bighorn sheep.

"Look at all those fools over there," their dad said, pointing to the packed parking lot full of tourists across the canyon. "And here we are on this side all by ourselves."

As was their custom, they sang to warn any bears in the area of their presence. But they rarely got all the way through a song. They could never remember all the lyrics and once Danielle started mangling them as only she could, the songs usually ended in an argument or a laugh.

"Wow," their dad said slowly, scanning the horizon. "Those bad boys look like they mean business."

Although it was still mostly blue overhead, dark clouds had gathered in the distance. A few minutes later they reached the turnaround point. A marmot poked its nose out of a nearby hole. It stood on a rock and studied them. A cold breeze blew from the north. It was time to head back.

Without talking, they instinctively picked up the pace. The sky had quickly turned the color of wet concrete. They were less than two miles from the car when the storm hit them like a blitzing linebacker blindsiding a defenseless quarterback. First wind and then rain. Emily had to hold on to her hat to keep it from being blown off her head. The big drops struck them from the side. In less than a minute, half of Emily's body was completely soaked while the other half, the side facing away from the canyon, was bone dry. Goose bumps engulfed her bare arms.

"April showers bring May flowers," Danielle whined. "Over someone's *grave*."

"Nice sentiment," Emily shouted, trying to smile. "Too bad it's June, you little goon."

But she knew how her sister felt. The suddenness and strength of the storm was scary. Their car felt very far away. The natural beauty of the place had made it clear and now the storm was hammering the point home: they were definitely not in Southern California anymore.

Since the morning began clear and this was such a short hike, their dad had left his daypack behind, bringing only a water bottle. The cheap, plastic ponchos sat nice and dry–and useless–in the trunk of the car.

The wind and the rain continued and were soon joined by thunder. At first the flashes of lightning and cracks of thunder were separated by several seconds. But the electrical part of the storm was coming their way.

Emily knew that the trail was their ticket back to the car. But on it they were exposed and taking a terrible beating. It also made them the highest point in the area. Not a good thing with lightning closing in. The nearby grove of Douglas fir down the hill looked cozy, but it probably did to bears as well. Not to mention that the trees would be powerful lightning magnets. The best thing would be to hunker down in the open ground between the canyon rim and the trees. But that brought with it the risk of hypothermia.

There didn't seem to be a good choice in sight.

"Come on!" their dad shouted as he stepped off the trail. Emily hesitated at first but followed, not knowing what else to do.

It was dark under the trees, very dark. But at least it gave them some shelter and a chance to re-group. Thunder exploded overhead as they huddled together.

"They're going t-t-to-to find our bones here," Danielle cried, her lips beginning to turn a little blue.

"I'm sorry, guys," their father said. "This is my fault. We should always bring rain gear. And I should have read the clouds better. Hot chocolate for everyone when we get back to town."

"If we g-g-get back," Danielle stammered.

Emily suddenly found herself staring down at a pile of bear scat. There were pine nuts in it. And it was steaming. She began shaking.

Stories from the bear attack book ripped through her mind. The woman who had been running on a trail with two friends before a bear tore into her.

The boy pulled out of a tent and dragged off to his death, his screams disappearing into the night. Another woman going on the roof of her cabin to escape a bear. The bear following her. Three teenage boys stalked and killed by a bear while fishing. Their bodies found together under a pile of leaves, the bear hovering over them, protecting its kill.

A grizzly hadn't killed anyone in Yellowstone in more than 20 years and the chances were much greater of dying from a bee sting or lightning or, under these conditions, hypothermia for sure. But out here at this point, the nearest bee felt even farther away than that hot chocolate, while man-killing bears lurked just a few feet away in the dark corners just beyond Emily's imagination, just beyond the next tree.

"Daaad," Emily called, the nightmare back and as fresh as the feces at her feet.

Just then a bright flash filled the forest followed almost immediately by another deafening roar overhead. With her ears ringing, her eyes desperately tried to adjust to the dark again. It was like coming out of a movie theater in the middle of a sunny afternoon. But the opposite. And worse.

Suddenly, Emily saw a large shape lumbering toward them from the far end of the grove. She couldn't be sure what she really saw, if anything, but at that moment she felt a terror no horror movie could match. She clenched her teeth to hold back the scream that had swallowed her mind.

"We've got to get moving," their dad shouted. "This is no good."

He grabbed Danielle by the hand and began running downhill. Emily didn't hesitate this time. She was too scared to look back. The storm was still raging. The thunder and lightning continued their assault. But in a few minutes, with the blood pumping hard through her body, Danielle had stopped shivering and her lips were no longer blue. Emily felt better too. She hoped the bear, whether flesh and blood or phantom of her imagination, was somewhere far behind them.

Like the rain, they kept dropping down and eventually reached a road. They started walking in the direction of the parking lot.

As the storm began to subside, a pickup truck pulled up beside them and the old man behind the wheel leaned across the wrinkled woman sitting next to him and asked, "What have you done here?"

"Just trying to avoid the tourists," their dad said.

The old man shook his head and pointed to the truck bed. They climbed in and in a few minutes were back at their car, cranking the heater and smiling and singing another song they would never finish.

***

As the bear ate some ants and wet pine nuts, he thought about the animals that had passed through his home a few moments earlier. There was something about these strange creatures that filled the bear with a curious, unfamiliar feeling. He imagined that it was what he saw in the eyes of the animals that became his food before he clawed and spilled the life out of them.

Maybe it was the way they walked, standing up on their back legs. Maybe it was the strange sounds they made. But they smelled good. Their scent still filled the air. It smelled better than huckleberries and trout and baby elk.

"Maybe next time I will taste that meat," he thought as thick saliva started to fill his mouth. "Maybe next time."

Dead Fall

Diego's grandfather fell to his death almost 20 years before Diego was born. He had been working on the barn roof. A slip, a misstep, and down, down, down he went. In the boy's imagination his *abuelito* had never stopped falling. In real life, of course, the ground had broken his fall. Broken so many things. Diego's father, a teenager at the time, had been standing a few feet away holding the ladder.

His dad never talked about it. But his mother did once. Late one night when his father had been away on business, she had wondered out loud if he had been blamed for the accident. If he blamed himself. If that was why he never talked to or visited his family back in Mexico.

"What an awful, terrible weight that must be to carry around," she had said, putting down her infomercial super weight-loss *té chino* and hugging herself.

Sometimes Diego would picture his dad as a 13- or 14-year-old boy standing by the plain pine open coffin, saying he was sorry. Or maybe not saying he was sorry. Maybe not saying anything. Some things are so bad, so horrible, that words like *lo siento* become small and useless and worse than silence. It's best to let some things die in the back of your throat, Diego thought.

The odd thing was that, scarred and tortured as he had to have been by the tragedy, his father was not afraid of heights. Standing near the top rung of a tall ladder to paint a high ceiling or looking down from the Golden Gate Bridge when they had visited San Francisco, he never showed the slightest hint of acrophobia. He didn't know if his grandfather had been scared. It didn't matter. Diego was scared enough for all three of them.

He wasn't certain if there was a connection that ran through the years between him and his falling grandfather, but for as long as Diego could remember, he had been afraid of heights. Maybe he had just been born that way. Maybe it was a combination of the two. Whatever the true cause, Diego got the sweats just standing on a chair or even looking at a Ferris wheel. Maybe that's why he couldn't get too far off the court when he was playing basketball. His friends joked that he had the worst case of white man's burden anyone had ever seen. Maybe it was something more.

But here he was now. Looking up at Half Dome. The granite monolith towered over Yosemite Valley and dealt a fatal blow to Diego's confidence, ripping it out of him like a punch to the stomach sucks out air. He stared at the cable staircase running up the monstrous boulder that had become a permanent fixture in his nightmares. As vivid as those dreams were, they had not prepared him for this moment.

He looked at the cables. And the cables looked into him.

He had been drawn to this place. Drawn to this challenge like a bug to a light bulb, like Icarus to the sun. From the first time he had seen a photograph of Half Dome at his middle school library back in Merced and read nervously about the cables and the hike, it would not leave his mind. He was haunted by it. Then one day he decided that he would do it. Just decided. He trained and practiced and got himself into shape for the 16-mile, 4800-foot climb.

Diego was still having trouble catching his breath even though he had been sitting for almost 10 minutes. His knees were shaking, palms wet. He was cold. Cold and scared.

Above him a few people were slowly making their way down. In the time that Diego had been there, another hiker had started up without hesitation. Then a man came up and sat down on a nearby rock.

"Pretty scary, huh?" he said.

"Yeah," Diego nodded, trying not to sound as scared as he felt. "Pretty scary."

The two of them sat there for a while, not speaking. Finally, the man rose.

"Well, I didn't come this far to turn back," he said. "See you at the top."

Diego gave him a thin cartoon smile and pulled the gloves out of his pack, pretending he was getting ready. In truth, he was giving serious thought to just turning around and giving up. He took another sip of water and looked up.

Somewhere deep inside he still had the desire, *las ganas*. Trouble was, that feeling was buried beneath a rockslide of fear. It gripped him and pinned him down.

Diego had done a few other hard things in his life. Facing down that bully back in 5th grade. Trying to figure out algebra and talk to girls or talk algebra and figure out girls. Either way, those things were hard for sure.

Watching his dog die had been hard too. She didn't die right away like his grandfather. She had died slowly. Little by little, piece by piece, the cancer had killed all the things she loved. She stopped running after her chewed-up tennis ball. She stopped eating her crunchy food pellets. Near the end she wouldn't even lick the empty ice cream container Diego would place by her head. She was really already dead by the time the vet stopped her heart and closed her confused, sad eyes for the last time.

Diego had not cried. For a long time he just felt empty. Empty and numb. A few weeks later he was finishing up a bowl of *dulce de leche* ice cream and noticed she wasn't there waiting at his feet, always waiting, her patience betrayed by a small drop of drool now and then. It was then that the tears came. Taking the place of the absent drool, the tears came hard.

But eventually the pain of her death faded and the memories of the way she was before came back. Like the time she was running after seagulls at the beach. Stopping suddenly at the water's edge to answer nature's call. Frozen in that photo-finish, race-horse pose she had at such moments. Offerings to Poseidon, the brown *caca* chunks dropped from her. Little memories like that.

Diego was sorry he didn't have happy memories of his *abuelo*. How could you remember what you never knew?

"Didn't come this far to turn back," he repeated. "Didn't come this far to turn back."

He said it again and again like a mantra, like a prayer. Each time with more feeling. Suddenly Diego felt his legs taking him toward the foot of the cables. He looked up and could see the portion of the climb high above that steepened to a 45-degree angle. Beyond that the trail disappeared.

Beyond that was the top.

"Didn't come this far to turn back," Diego whispered, his mouth as dry as baby powder.

He took one step and squeezed the cable. Another step. And another handful of cable. Inside his gloves he could feel the sweat pooling. He looked down at the rock. His whole world was granite gray now. Every once in a while a two-by-four step broke up the sameness. Out of the corner of his eye he could see the blue sky that made up the rest of the world but he didn't dare look at it. He just kept snailing his way up. He was not aware of the thin air or the sheerness of the climb or how far he had come or how far he still had to go. All he focused on was that one step.

Secure three, move one, he told himself. One step. One handhold. One step. One handhold. Secure three, move one.

One step.

At one point a shadow came toward him. Gripping one of the cables with both hands, he moved to one side of the narrow staircase to let the descending hikers pass. He wouldn't want to have to step aside like this too often. Diego was glad he had gotten an early start. It would not be pretty to be up here when it was crowded.

Only a handful of people had died while climbing this section over the years. And now Diego knew why. The cables took every bit of concentration you had. There was little chance of being distracted. Still, he could also see the other side of it: how it would be possible and easy to fall. Very easy. And once you started falling, it would be hard to stop. He quickly pushed the demon, the specter of falling, over the edge of his consciousness.

"Quite a view up there," one of the hikers said, as Diego's left quad started shaking. "You're almost there."

He smiled and nodded without looking up and continued climbing.

The cable part of the hike gained just over 400 feet. Four hundred feet on a flat surface wasn't very far. Not much beyond a 100-yard dash. Little more than a football field. But up here, as Diego inched his way up, it felt like a great distance. Still, he got into a rhythm–a very slow rhythm–and at a point much sooner than he would have expected, the trail started to lose some of its steepness. It was starting to flatten out.

Looking up for the first time since he started, Diego saw the end. His pace quickened and soon the cables were behind him. A few easy, sweet minutes later, he was on top. On top of Half Dome. On top of the world! He had done it! He had done it!

He looked around and saw Yosemite Valley far below and El Capitan and he took out his hiking book to identify Clouds Rest and Cathedral Peak and Mt. Hoffman but quickly put it away. This moment wasn't about names. It was about the feeling. *Hijole*, what a feeling! That inner glow kept him warm against the chilly mid-day breeze hitting his sweaty T-shirt.

It was amazing how flat and huge it was on top. Little squirrels ran around nervously. They must live their whole lives up here, Diego thought. Nuts. Or maybe they followed the hikers up, knowing a meal ticket when they saw one. He took some pictures, including a couple of arms-length self-portraits. Then he sat on a rock and drank an orange-colored sports drink and ate a candy bar. His head wouldn't stop doing 360s. After a while he stood up. Clouds were gathering on the horizon. It was time to head back.

It was funny how he didn't even feel the least bit scared now. His eyes took in everything they had missed on the way up and he started his descent of the cables with no trace of fear. A feeling of happiness and pride pushed all other emotions out of his heart. The stairway didn't even seem all that steep, the way it had coming up.

Suddenly Diego's shadow disappeared from the rock. A passing cloud, thick and dark, covered the sun. The smooth granite soon turned silver and slick with rain, but Diego could see that most of the world below was still brightly lit in sunshine. He smiled at the thought of buying one of those T-shirts he had seen that said, "I Hiked Half Dome." He smiled and took another step.

His left foot slipped on the wet rock. A split second later his right hand missed the cable. Suddenly Diego was falling.

Falling.

Falling.

His arms and legs flailing and missing and bouncing and sliding off the rock.

Falling.

Falling.

Like his grandfather.

Rock and sky tumbled and blurred and time slowed down and sped up again. And Diego fell. The last chance support post flew by and he found himself outside the cables now and his fingers caught hold of air, more air, just air, and then . . . somehow . . . metal.

His shoulder almost came out of its socket from the strain of the sudden, violent stop but his fingers held. They held and Diego let go a long sigh, grabbing the pole with both hands. He was bruised and bloodied in places, but incredibly he had not broken anything. He stayed there for a long time breathing and gripping the steel and hugging the granite. Breathing. Just breathing.

He finally stood up, nodded slowly at the sky, and made his way down the rest of the staircase.

As he hiked the long, dusty trail back to the valley floor, Diego was thoroughly sore and exhausted. But happy. No, it was something beyond happiness.

He couldn't remember the air ever tasting so good or being so alive with promise and possibility.

The thought occurred to him that he had been given a second chance. The chance his grandfather never had. He decided he would do important things with his life. He would start by talking to that girl in his math class when he got back to school. He started going over what he would say and laughed out loud because he knew he was talking nonsense. It didn't matter.

Passing the hordes of tourists he met as he closed in on the trailhead, Diego found himself smiling at everyone and everything. His knee was sore and caked in dry blood. His elbow too. But the blood had not come from his heart.

His heart was full.

Downriver with John

Out here on this muddy river that flows at a relaxed pace, the sun smashes into you. It's like a shovel to the back of the head sometimes.

"It's so hot," Paul said, lifting up his French Foreign Legion-style cap and wiping sweat off his forehead.

"We'll stop in the shade for lunch," his dad said.

They paddled over to the shore. Paul jumped out of the canoe first, pulling it up through gooey, brown mud. He was barefoot and the smelly slop squished between his toes. They walked with their lunch over to some shade.

"Did you know that outlaws in the 1800s used to hide out here in these canyons?" his dad said, not missing the chance to drop some history trivia on Paul.

They were paddling down the Green River in Utah, a place where massive red, brown, and orange walls flanked each side and huge rock formations and buttes made up the landscape in the distance. They could have been on Mars, Paul thought. It was so strange to stare out at these colors, so different from the grays and greens of Portland.

They watched the gurgling, coffee-colored water flow by as they demolished a box of peanut butter crackers. They would stay on the Green until it mixed into the Colorado River, 52 miles away. There, Paul and his dad would be picked up in a powerboat by the same outfitters who dropped them off earlier that morning. A few miles down from that point was Cataract Canyon, a series of seriously bone-chilling, white-knuckle Class V rapids that only expert rafters ran.

They headed back to the canoe and pushed off.

"Wow, it's hot," Paul said again.

Later in the afternoon, he took off his T-shirt, dunked it in the water, and put it back on. He did the same thing with his hat. After a few more hours of paddling, they found a large, sandy island in the middle of the river.

"Honey, we're home," his dad said.

Things were a little different camping in the sandy, slickrock river canyons of Utah. For one, you couldn't dig a hole for your toilet. Instead, campers had to pack in and pack out their solid waste in a small metal box. When the trip ended, the outfitters took away the rented toilets. It was pretty gross, Paul thought, that the park service made everyone carry that smelly box everywhere they went, but he didn't want to imagine how this place would be if they didn't have that rule.

After the tent was up, Paul chased down the Frisbee his dad fired his way. A slight breeze pushed down the canyon, which helped cool them off. They went swimming before dinner on the side where the river was shallow and slow and the water felt great. They dried off sitting in the sand, watching the sun fall behind a massive rock wall as a black raven circled above. ,

Dinner was summer sausage and cheese bread. Watching the light leave the sky, his dad told stories about Butch Cassidy and the Hole in the Wall Gang, previous residents of these canyons.

"We best turn in," his dad said. "We have a long day of paddling and hiking tomorrow."

No one had to tell Paul to get to bed. He was wiped!

They brought up the canoe and turned it over. While his dad tied down the gear, Paul peed one last time. This was another strange park service rule: all urine had to go in the river. Something about the bacteria not being able to break down on the sand or rocks. Paul stood at the edge of the island and tried not to think about it too much, especially because they had been swimming just a little while ago.

He unzipped the tent and bundled up into his slippery sleeping bag. It was amazing how cold it had gotten after being so hot during the day. Within minutes, he fell into a deep sleep.

***

As the sun rose, it ignited the orange and red sandstone across the river, turning the cliffs into a fiery blaze. Soon their small sandbar was at the mercy of the yellow beast. Paul was sweating as they packed up. While his dad loaded the canoe, he checked over the island, making sure they hadn't forgotten anything.

It was a big, blue cloudless morning. His dad guided them to spots along the river where they looked through binoculars and saw ancient drawings carved into the rocks called petroglyphs. Just past noon they pulled off and found the trail up to Moki Fort, a large Anasazi Indian ruin high above the river built of mud and thin rocks. It was supposed to be more than 800 years old.

"They sure knew about architecture," his dad said, standing next to the tower as Paul took his picture. "Built to last."

Paul looked down and was happy to get a different perspective of the river as it stretched off in the distance. This place was incredible. But the heat was suffocating.

"Must be over 100 degrees," his dad said. "We're not in Kansas anymore."

"What?"

They charged back down to the river and splashed their faces and dunked their hats and shirts before getting into the canoe.

They paddled on, stopping only once the rest of the afternoon. Finally, with the sun behind them and dropping, they found another sandy campsite and set up the tent.

Paul brought out his sketchpad and pencils. He sketched the landscape with two large buttes off in the distance. As they ate dinner, they talked about how great it would be to live in these canyons, how maybe some day they could become outfitters and take city folks out to the river. Soon bright stars scattered across the black sky, and they headed to bed.

***

The next morning they packed up slowly, drinking strong cowboy coffee in between breaking up camp and loading the canoe. It was cloudy and windy, but they were thankful that the sun was hidden.

"Something's coming in," Paul's dad said, studying the sky. "Let's get going."

Within an hour, the clouds had grown thick and by early afternoon, they were tombstone-gray dark.

"Whoa," Paul said as a fierce, howling wind shot into them from down the canyon. Big, cold raindrops fell and the river quickly turned angry, sending large waves over the bow. Water sloshed at their feet.

"Paul," his dad shouted over the wind. "This is getting dangerous. We need to get off the river. See any shoreline?"

Paul looked for a spot, but the thick tamarisk trees and huge rock walls made it impossible to pull off. He pushed his paddle deep into the water, making strong, full strokes. They paddled hard but made little progress against the wind that was trying to tip their canoe sideways into the water.

"Keep it going!" his dad yelled.

Suddenly, a shock of blinding bluish-white light lit up everything, followed by ear-shattering thunder that cracked the air around them. They both jumped.

"Shazam," his dad said. "That was nasty!"

Paul shook his head. He could feel blisters forming on his palms from gripping the paddle so hard. His heart pounded in his ears. His arms ached as he scanned the sides looking for any small bit of shoreline. Then he saw it.

"Over there, on the right," Paul yelled.

It was a small spot, but it would do if they could get to it in time. Another lightning and thunder combination jolted the canyon. The storm was nearly on top of them. They paddled hard against the choppy water.

They slammed into the sand, jumped out, and pulled up the canoe. They worked fast, tying down the boat and finding the raincoats. Paul's dad brought out the large, blue tarp and tied it to some branches, creating a little shelter. They huddled under their plastic sky and watched the chaos.

The storm made everything more vivid, more colorful and alive. The river churned in front of them, full of whitecaps flowing in the opposite direction. Numerous waterfalls developed on the rock walls across from them, cascading hundreds of feet down. As the thunder boomed mercilessly overhead, Paul was happy they had found this spot to watch the desert transform into a violent and beautiful place.

It wasn't until dusk that the rain stopped and the wind relaxed into a light breeze. They decided to stay put for the night, even though it wasn't a great campsite. There was just enough room for the tent. They had crackers, dried fruit, and large hunks of Parmesan cheese for dinner.

"Boy, this place is crazy!" Paul said.

The night wasn't cold at all, and Paul read some great scary stories from his favorite book before drifting off to sleep.

***

Paul was relieved to see a clear sky when he stepped out of the tent. The sun was still hidden behind the rock walls. He walked to the river to pee. When he came back, he found his dad studying the map.

"We really have to hit it hard today," he said, looking up. "We're a little behind because of the storm."

They got to work and pushed off just as the sun lit up the canyon. The river was back to its relaxed pace and the long hours of paddling were pleasant, although it was hot again. They didn't hike, but stopped a few times for breaks.

"We've done well today," his dad said. "But we'll get up early tomorrow to make sure we get to the pick-up point by noon. Don't want to miss those guys. I can't wait for an icy Coke!"

"And ice cream!" Paul said.

"And showers!" his dad shouted.

"Showers of ice cream!" Paul said.

"It's great out here though," he added, feeling a little sad that the trip was coming to an end. He sat while his dad assembled the cooking gear, thinking how much he would miss it. He felt something new in him, something he hadn't felt before. He knew he would be back. He had to. This was now a part of him. He belonged out here.

***

In the morning after breakfast, they packed up and put in for the last time. An hour later another river flowed in from the left.

"Dad? What river is this?"

When Paul turned around, he saw his dad looking at the map.

"Um, the Colorado is still a ways away," he said. "I'm guessing this is just an old meander that went around those cliffs over there and is meeting back up with the main channel that we are on. We're good. I see it on the map."

A few miles later, they saw a large wooden sign on a beach coming up on their right.

Suddenly there was wild thrashing in the water just ahead. Paul stared at the strange mixture of foam and living mud and his eyes went big.

"Snakes!" he yelled. "Snakes!"

With great insane sweeps of his paddle, he fought to steer the boat away from the swirling, snake-infested waters.

"Ease up there, lunatic!" his dad said, laughing at Paul's wild strokes. "They're just catfish!"

Paul looked closer and breathed a sigh of relief. He stopped paddling and studied the strange circle as they floated next to it for a while. He could see lots of fish mouths opening and closing at the surface. He also noticed that they had creepy, long mustaches. It was one of the weirdest things he had ever seen.

"Should we go back and see what that sign said?" Paul asked after a while.

"Well, according to the map, that's where a trail starts," his dad said. "The sign probably just talks about the hike."

They paddled on.

Paul thought of the motor boat that would be picking them up soon. He thought about the little town of Moab and hoped there was a cool ice cream shop where he could get a banana split.

"Our pullout must be just around that bend," his dad said.

But the sound of rushing water was around the bend instead. The river picked up speed. Paul could feel his heart trying to match it.

"Don't worry, Paul," his dad said. "It probably gets faster as we merge with the Colorado River, plus all the extra water from that storm."

It was a good theory, Paul thought. He pushed his paddle in but there was no need. The river was taking them. Up ahead the water roared.

Then the realization hit him all at once, falcon-fast but too slow to do anything about it. They weren't on the Green anymore. They were on the Colorado. Had been for a while. They had missed their take-out point. They were heading down Cataract Canyon!

"Rapids, Dad! Up ahead!" Paul shouted.

"Reverse! Back paddle!" his dad yelled.

They tried, but it was useless. The current was too strong and it pulled them down into some of the most intense whitewater on earth.

His dad shouted something as the roar became deafening. What it was, Paul could not say. The muddy water sloshed into the canoe, drenching Paul, filling the bottom. Large, brown waves came at them from all sides. They bounced right into a huge monster wall of water, rode over the top okay but as they plunged down, Paul flew out the side and–splash!–he was in the river. He saw the canoe shoot up like a wounded rocket, and smash back into the water upside down. Their gear scattered in the waves. Another huge wave pummeled Paul, pulling him under and pinning him there. He couldn't get to the surface. He held his breath, hitting and kicking furiously at the water. His mind screamed for a miracle.

Suddenly the silver toilet struck him in the chest. Paul grabbed hold and it blasted him up to the top. He inhaled in quick gasps. He could breathe! And he wasn't far from shore. He saw his dad, glasses gone, trying to stay afloat behind him.

"Dad! Over here! Grab hold of the toilet!"

His dad lunged for the metal box and they both held on, kicking over to a nearby eddy. Sweet relief flooded through them as they pulled themselves out of the mouth of the muddy rapids. They threw themselves down in the sand, breathing hard under the hot sun.

"Paul! I think we went down Brown Betty, the first part of Cataract Canyon!" his dad said after a few minutes. "How in the name of John Wesley Powell did that happen?"

"I don't know," Paul said. "But that toilet saved us. Our smelly toilet saved us!"

They laughed loud and hard, their cackling echoing off the red canyon walls and blending with the ferocious river.

Paul smiled and squinted in the sun, staring at his dad, whose face–all flustered and confused–looked like a giant, red question mark.

Round and Round

January 18, 2:30 p.m.

The wind, sounding like lonely wolves on a hollow night, blows hard through the trees, blasting icy shards into their puffy, frozen faces. Everything is gray and white. There is no yellow sun, no blue sky, no green trees, no clear trail. It has all disappeared in a murky, colorless moment.

They lumber up a hillside, hard going in the thick, powdery snow. Big clumps of white fall from the trees, occasionally smacking them in the head. Their breath leaks out in ghostly wisps over the frozen landscape.

"Haven't we been here before?" Kathryn says. "This looks familiar."

Her fingers and toes are stinging and she claps her gloved hands together to fight off the cold. Her mouth is as dry as a fossil. She reaches for her water bottle.

"I don't think so, but let me take a look," Ryan says.

He jams his poles deep into the snow and takes off his pack. He pulls out the map and grips it as the wind tries to tear it from his hands.

"The shelter's around here," he says.

"Yeah, but where are *we*?" she asks, staring at the map flapping wildly.

Ryan doesn't know exactly where they are. What he does know is that they have been walking for two hours and should have been at the wooden shelter by now. But their progress has been slow because of the fresh snow. As he looks at the map, he worries that they have veered off trail into the massive backcountry of the Three Sisters wilderness.

"I think we're here," Ryan says, pointing it out. "So we shouldn't be too far. It would be good to get there and rest a little before heading back to the car."

"Okay, I'm gonna call home," Kathryn says, grabbing her cell phone.

Ryan knows before she says it.

"No service," she says.

"It's the trees. When we get out into the open, it'll work."

Kathryn has done a lot of hiking in these mountains with her dad, but always in the summer. She has even been on this trail and to the small hut they are heading toward. But everything looks so different in the snow. So different in its sameness.

"I saw that shelter last July," she says. "It has a large wood stove."

Ryan folds the map.

"Let's get going."

3:05 p.m.

"Break," Kathryn yells through the ruthless wind. They stop and slide off their packs. Their faces are bright red.

"Man, it wasn't supposed to be like this," Ryan says. "The weatherman promised sunny skies."

"Well, it'll make a good story for when we get back," Kathryn says.

Ryan looks around.

"We haven't seen anyone for hours." The minute he says this, he wishes he hadn't. "But maybe they are at the shelter, warming up."

Kathryn shivers, her teeth chattering like a skeleton gone crazy on Halloween night.

3:20 p.m.

Ryan's leg muscles are tight and sore. With each plodding step, his doubts grow. Pretty soon they will grow legs of their own. He wonders if they should just try to make it back to the car, which is in the opposite direction. Or is it?

Ryan is good at focusing. Soccer has taught him that. But out here he has to remind himself to focus on what he wants. *See it in your mind*, his coach says.

He sees them sitting next to a raging fire, happy and warm.

3:50 p.m.

In these winter woods filled with snow, filled with snow and unspoken prayers, the lightness is bleeding from the sky. These winter woods make for long nights and one of those long, long nights is making its way toward Ryan and Kathryn.

"I think it's time to get back to the car," Ryan says. He sees the day fading and knows that finding that shelter now is useless.

"Yeah," Kathryn says. "Good idea."

She sighs into the new shadows as they turn around. The snow now falls in large, feathery flakes.

3:54 p.m.

Out in the open, it doesn't work either.

"Must be the clouds," he says.

She puts the phone back in her pocket.

4:15 p.m.

Kathryn thinks about a lot of things as she pushes lead-like legs in and out of the snow. She thinks about her parents, about how much she wishes she were home with them now. She thinks about her friends, who had laughed when she told them she was going snowshoeing with Ryan. They wanted to know why they weren't doing something cooler, like snowboarding or skiing. Sometimes, she thinks, she hates those friends.

She also thinks about how it's getting dark, about how the snow just keeps falling, about how they certainly seem to be lost. Very, very lost.

4:30 p.m.

Kathryn grabs the phone, pushes a button, and waits. They walk on.

"It's so c-c-c-oooold," she says. The last part blows away into the darkening hills.

4:47 p.m.

They probably have been walking in circles all afternoon, Kathryn thinks. There are no landmarks. Just white in all directions. Different shades of white. Soon, she thinks, they'll be white too.

4:50 p.m.

The sun—wherever it is—is about to set.

"I've been thinking about it," Ryan says. "If we don't find the car or the hut we'll have to spend the night out here. But we'll be okay. We'll dig one of those snow caves like mountain climbers dig when a storm comes in."

Kathryn can't believe that this is happening.

"I'll make us a fire too," Ryan says. "I have a box of matches and a lot of fire-starter and we'll dig up some branches and twigs near the trees. Let's keep going until six. Then we'll stop and set up camp. We're going to get out of this. I promise."

Kathryn likes the idea of a fire. She can't feel her toes or fingers anymore.

4:59 p.m.

"I know it was smoke," Ryan says. "I know I smelled smoke."

Kathryn inhales deeply.

"I just smell cold," she says.

Tree after tree, nothing but deep snow and now something new. Darkness.

5:15 p.m.

Kathryn's face isn't red anymore, more like an ash white, and this scares Ryan. She is so little out here. While he knows he can survive a freezing night in this wilderness, he isn't sure she can.

"We'll be okay, Kathryn," he says in a quiet voice.

As he walks, he envisions touching the wood shingles on that hut. Inside is glorious. Orange flames and heat. Soothing smoke wraps around them tightly as they sit on a wooden bench, laughing about the close call. The fire brings life back to their numb bodies.

Snap. Back to reality. "Kathryn?"

Kathryn is sitting on the ground, looking like a beaten dog.

"Hey!" he yells into the blackness, into the wind, into the continuous falling snow that piles around them.

Anger shoots through his body. He's angry that he has taken them out on this horrible trip, angry that he has led them to the middle of nowhere, angry that he can't find that idiotic shelter or even the car. But he is now mostly angry at Kathryn for sitting in the snow, waiting to die.

"Kathryn. Get up. Get up!" he screams. "Are you just going to lay down and die?"

5:15 p.m.

Her exhaustion is brutal.

Kathryn needs to sit, anywhere, and in fact does just that, in the middle of the snowfield they are crossing.

"Get up!" Ryan yells at her. "Get up! Are you just going to lay down and die?"

Kathryn stares up at Ryan with frozen eyes.

117

9:30 p.m.

It has finally stopped snowing and the wind has blown out. The landscape is strange, moon-like. Bright stars sparkle above. The woods are black, except for the fire.

They have dug a small snow cave for later.

"It's so quiet out here," Kathryn says. She is better now, her face a good color, the starkness gone, her eyes alert.

At times it feels as if they are on a first date sitting in a booth at the diner. They exchange bits of information about each other: their families, favorite music, movies they like. They talk about bad teachers and kids at school. They talk about their futures, both wanting to live in a big city.

Ryan and Kathryn have hopes of a good night, of keeping this fire going, of staying alive. The night will be long and hard. But they can almost touch the sunlight they see in their minds, feel the heat from its glow, inhale the brightness of the morning sky.

Too Much Five-O

David sat in the back seat stuffing *Krispy Kremes* into his face.

"Go easy on those," his dad said. "The road up ahead is supposed to get pretty gnarly and I don't want you blowing donut chunks all over the rental car."

"Yeah, okay," David said, thinking his old man was quite lame trying to sound so surfer dude hip and all.

It turned out his dad was right though. There were some pretty nasty turns on the road to Hana. His dad drove slower than frozen peanut butter but those curves still shook up David's stomach something awful.

"Ooooaaaaahhhh," he moaned, turning as green as some of the vegetation outside his window.

In parts the "highway" was just one lane. The senseless freaks in the oncoming convertibles were oblivious to the concept of sharing the road. They torpedoed right for the car as his dad swerved the *Krispy Kremes* out of the way just in time, time and time again.

The Hana Highway was only about 50 miles long. But on this day, David would learn that distance wasn't always something measured in miles.

Somehow the car's upholstery survived. And they did too. There were even T-shirts at the souvenir shops you could buy to prove it.

David's stomach began to come back to life as he smelled the sweet tropical plants along the last fairly straight stretch of the road before the town of Hana. He saw cows and horses up on the hillside.

"Anyone up for a burger?" his dad asked. "They're supposed to have some dead meat done right at this stand up ahead."

"No freakin' way," David thought. "No freakin' way, *brah*."

He just wanted to get back in the water. Tomorrow they would be boarding a plane back to the mainland. He wanted to experience H_2O in its warmer, liquid form as much as possible before returning to his snow- and ice-covered corner of the world.

Catching nasty stink eye from some of the locals, David walked down the road while he waited for his parents and sister to finish their lunch. His mind filled with fish of all shapes and colors and giant turtles, like the ones he had seen while snorkeling on the other side of Maui during the past few days.

"Now remember, Wavy Davy," his dad warned when they got down to the beach. "This side of the island takes no prisoners–those babies can get *mondo humongous*."

Yeah, the waves looked big all right. No ankle busters here. Hitting the shore in irregular sets of four, they were pretty epic as far as David could tell. But if things got too intense he would just swim back, he thought. Other people were out. There was one teenage girl who kept getting whaled upon as she tried to boogie board. David watched her for a while, hoping the waves would readjust her bathing suit.

After a few minutes, he took off his aloha shirt and ran for the water. He mistimed his entrance and got hammered right off the bat. He picked himself up, hoping the girl hadn't seen his moment of utter feebleness. But it didn't take him too long to recover his confidence and feel at home in the water.

"Yaw!" he shouted. "Ride 'em, cowboy!"

David rose and fell with each swell as it passed under him. He swam out past the third wave so that there was just one left between him and the open ocean. Far enough, he thought. He swam effortlessly on his back for a while and looked up at the clear, blue November sky. The sun made the water sparkle.

A few minutes later, he decided it was time to head back to shore. On the beach his family seemed very far away and David saw that he was farther out than any of the other people in the water. That burger began to sound good. He started swimming back.

After a short time, he looked up and noticed he was in the same place or possibly even farther away from the beach. Maybe it was just the salt water distorting his vision, he thought. Still, a small wave of panic swept across his mind. *Ain't no big ting, braddah*, a voice said in his head sounding like Chin Ho Kelly on a rerun of Hawaii Five-0. No need to *get up pretty tight*, Kono counseled. Yeah, stay cool like Steve McGarrett, David told himself. Put the cuffs on this fear and *book 'em, Dano*. He would just have to swim a little harder, was all. He took a deep breath.

He wished he had the fins he had used while snorkeling. But they were back at the rental shop on the other side of the island. Still, he gave it everything he had. He kicked at the water furiously for what seemed like several minutes. His arms and lungs ached from the effort. When he glanced up, David again noticed that he hadn't made any progress. In fact, he was sure the shore was farther away than ever. The waves were even larger and doing their best to help him back to shore, but the rip current was even stronger. He was swimming as hard as he could and he was still being pulled out to sea. Out to sea!

Everything had been so peaceful when he had been snorkeling. It was like swimming in a giant aquarium. The ocean had lulled him into a false sense of security.

He was like one of those boxers facing Muhammad Ali in his prime. The way he would hypnotize them with that windmill motion of one arm and then rock them with a lightning-quick jab from the other. Except Ali did it mostly for effect and showmanship. He didn't inflict much damage with that move, except to his opponent's pride. The difference here was that the ocean wasn't playing around. Not today. David suddenly knew there was much more at stake than pride.

The pounding of his heart was as loud as the surf. It beat as much now from the fear that ripped through it as from the exertion of the swim. He waved to his parents frantically. They waved back. But did nothing. *Do you think I'm just being friendly? No! Help! Help!*

"Help!" he shouted at the top of his lungs. "Hel . . . "

Before he could finish the word, a huge wave crashed down on him from behind. Water poured into his open mouth. He swallowed some and gasped. The stinging salt water backed up in his nose as he wheezed and coughed.

He felt as helpless as he did when he went to the dentist. Hanging upside down in that chair, with all those instruments of torture in his mouth and his saliva working overtime and his heart going nuts.

"Try to relax," the dentist would say. "Just relax."

David just wanted to relax all the way out the door and run as fast and as far away as he could. How good it would be to be on dry land right now. Running. Running, running, running away from the sea.

His heart felt on the verge of exploding. The terror had torn a Titanic-size gash in him. Whatever energy he had left was spilling out at an alarming rate. His muscles had tightened into useless knots. He felt his body weaken and his will waver. Meanwhile, the ocean just seemed to be getting stronger.

He knew he had to try again. Again he attacked the strongest force on earth head on, doing his best to make some progress. He pushed against the water and the suffocating pain in his lungs and legs. But it was no use.

He saw his dad run into the water and start swimming toward him.

"Too late, dad!" David's mind screamed. "Too late!"

Panic shot through every cell in his body now like an electric current. The muscles in his calves were thrashed. They cramped up and he went under. At first he held his breath and used his arms to swim up to the surface.

Then another big wave came and he swallowed more water. When he gasped this time his mouth dropped below the surface and took in still more water. Choking and coughing and desperately trying to suck in some air, he burst above the surface again, long enough to see his father and another swimmer getting closer now. Again he went down. His legs and arms were jelly. He had nothing left.

David held his breath as long as he could. Jolts of pain racked his brain. The pressure in his chest was unbearable. Finally, he began screaming underwater. Water poured into his lungs.

In the terrible moments that followed, David lost all sense of time. But at some point, the pain and the panic swam away. All he felt now was exhaustion. But it was a good tired, like finally hitting the pillow after a long day at soccer camp. His eyes saw *Krispy Kreme*-colored coral and fish. The boogie board girl was down there too. She smiled and waved and he wondered how she could be breathing down here and how he could be breathing down here and how anyone could like Cristiano Ronaldo.

Then the sun above the water's surface began to turn black and a neon dolphin swam by. The donuts and the dolphin and the girl called to David. His eyes were closed now. But he could still see everything. He even saw himself, drifting down toward them. Drifting down into the darkness that was enveloping him.

Something grabbed David's limp arm. But it didn't feel like his arm anymore. It felt like a part of him he no longer needed. He didn't need anything now. No fins. No burger. No window seat on the airplane.

Everything turned to black . . .

Winter . . . Summer

The snow kept falling. And falling. There was nothing to do except shiver. The world was white and cold, and it felt to Chuck that it had always, and would always, be that way.

He slept and dreamt of the wood stove and his bed and playing basketball inside a hot, smelly gym and pepperoni pizza. The emptiness that had started in his stomach was growing by the hour, taking over more and more of his body and mind. Soon the emptiness would be all that was left of him . . .

***

The wind was really blowing now. Whitecaps covered the water. Jacob was glad he was close to shore. Wouldn't want to be out in the middle of the lake with this thing blowing.

He paddled over to the shore, jumped out, and dragged the kayak over the smooth rock shelf. He dug into his daypack and fished out the map. Nothing on the map matched up to real life. He had to be lost. This giant lake didn't seem to be near where he should be or thought he should be. Nowhere near. The map made no sense to him as it danced in the wind. He took out his compass and lined up north with north on the map. It still didn't add up. He had no idea where he was. No idea.

He reached for the cell phone in the small outer pocket of the pack. There was a slight chance he could get reception out here. Even if he couldn't tell them exactly where he was, at least he could let his parents know he was safe. They would be expecting him soon and he knew how his mom liked to worry. Okay, maybe she didn't like to worry. She just seemed to spend a lot of time doing it.

Jacob hoped they wouldn't be too mad. He had said he could handle it, that he could spend the day on his own and meet them at the night's campsite. It was the sixth day of their 90-mile loop trip through the Boundary Waters and Quetico and he was 12, not some little kid, and he knew what he was doing. They had trusted him. And now he was lost.

He ducked into the trees to get out of the wind and punched *2* on his contact list. "No Network" was all that came up. He tried a couple more times with the same result.

At least the wind was good for something, he thought as he turned back toward the water. It kept away the biting buffalo gnats and those man-eating mosquitoes that had tortured him during certain parts of the trip.

But returning to shore, Jacob was immediately confronted with evidence that the wind was *good* for another thing too. The kayak wasn't where he had left it. He looked both ways, like a pedestrian crossing a street. No kayak. Then he glanced out on the whipped-up lake and saw it, about 100 feet out and getting farther away by the second. The wind had blown it into the water.

"Think," his mind said. "Think fast!"

But no thoughts came. Trying to swim after it seemed out of the question. The wind was too strong. He would not catch up to it, just be lured out into the huge lake.

Jacob stood there mouthing "no, no, no" and watching the kayak get smaller and smaller as the gusts pushed it across the choppy water.

"Now what?" his mind screamed. "Now *what*!"

Again, he had no answer. Maybe the wind would stop or shift and the yellow kayak would magically blow back to where he was standing. That might happen if he were a character in a fairy tale, he thought. But this was real life. All too real. And he was in it up to his ears. His big, *Dopey* ears.

***

Chuck's grandfather had given him the camera for Christmas. It was an ancient, non-digital one just like the old man had. Chuck loved to sit in the basement darkroom and watch the images come to life in the chemical-filled trays and listen to his grandfather talk about basketball in the old days.

"Most of these players today are just big babies, not men," he would say. "Walt 'Clyde' Frazier, Earl 'The Pearl' Monroe, 'The Big O,' Bill Russell–now those were men. They were men on and off the court. They lived basketball and lived by a code."

Chuck was a fan of the San Antonio Spurs even though he lived in Minnesota. His favorite player was Manu Ginóbili. He was left handed, just like Chuck.

"That kid's all right," his grandfather would say. "Got a lot of heart. Timmy Duncan too."

Sometimes his grandfather would work for hours and hours in the darkroom and not have anything to show for it. Then suddenly he would slap Chuck on the back and shout, "Now that one's a keeper!"

Chuck couldn't wait to go out and shoot some pictures in the woods near his home. His dad had said he would take him when he had some time but Chuck knew that it could be a while. He didn't want to wait.

So the Monday after Christmas he got up early and loaded his backpack with film and water and a few candy bars. He went outside and strapped on his snowshoes. It was cold and clear and the forest called to him.

Chuck walked deeper and deeper into the woods, at some point crossing into the Boundary Waters wilderness that was near the house. The camera felt right in his hands as he snapped off some shots of rabbit tracks disappearing in the sparkling, white background. Snow began falling as he switched on the flash and turned the camera on himself. He liked how the flash froze the flakes in midair, transforming them into popcorn, cotton ball splotches of white.

He stopped under a tree to have a chocolate bar. He sat down and thought about some of the pictures he had taken. Even though he wouldn't know for sure until the photos were developed, he felt he had a few "keepers" in the mix. A chill ripped through his jacket. He looked up and noticed that the snow was really coming down now and the wind was blowing hard from the north. He needed to start heading back.

Chuck pulled the hood drawstrings on his jacket tight and kept his head down, trying to protect the exposed skin on his face from the biting wind as much as possible and still see. Not that he could see much. The snow was so thick that it was hard to make out more than a few feet in front of him.

***

The gathering clouds were getting darker by the second. The sky was going to open up any moment now. Thunder was already rumbling in the distance. Jacob reached into his pack and pulled out the cheap, paper-thin emergency poncho.

He felt dumb as he put it on. He knew now–knew now like Kurt Warner knew now he shouldn't have thrown that pass in the Super Bowl–that he should have secured the kayak better, tied it off to a tree or a large rock. But he was only going to be away for a minute. No more than a minute.

"I'm so stupid," he said to the wind, fighting back tears. "Stupid, stupid, *stuuuupid*."

***

The hours passed and the snow fell hard and Chuck kept moving, back toward his house. Except nothing looked familiar and he wasn't so sure anymore that he was heading in the right direction. He should have seen a few houses by now. But all there was was forest and field and frozen lakes and snow on the ground and snow in the air. The storm went on without end, but the winter day was drawing to a close.

Chuck had been fighting the thought that he might have to spend the night out here. It would probably get down in the teens tonight. He was dressed for the cold, but it still didn't sound like fun.

It was getting darker and darker and Chuck now had to face the fact that he wasn't anywhere near his house. He had to admit to himself that he didn't know where he was or where his home was.

It didn't make much sense to plow on in the dark. The smart thing to do would be to find a place to spend the night and start again in the morning. He was a little scared at the thought but being exhausted from the long day of breaking trail through fresh snow helped. He was too tired to feel much fear. It would be good to stop.

He looked around in the dying light for a good place to dig. He had seen enough of those survival shows on TV to know that a snow cave would be a good idea. He found a spot under a thick white cedar and began using one of his snowshoes to dig. It didn't take too long to hollow out a trench long enough for his body to fit into. Then he started collecting branches for the floor and to place on top to support the snow for the roof.

When he finished he slid in feet first to try it out. It wasn't bad but he didn't want to stay in just yet. He didn't have his watch but he knew that with the daylight almost gone, it had to be about four. It wouldn't be light again for more than 15 hours. The night would be long as it was and Chuck didn't want to make it any longer. He crawled back out and stood under a tree, watching the snow fall.

It was the longest night of Chuck's life. It felt like he slept a total of 10 minutes. The rest of the time he spent tossing and turning and fighting off cramps in his calves. He wasn't exactly warm, but he wasn't as cold as he would have thought either.

It was still snowing hard when Chuck removed the backpack, which he had used as a door, and poked his head outside. As he looked at the clearing he had come from, he couldn't see any signs of his tracks. The snow had covered everything.

He walked around for a bit and painted the snow with dark yellow urine. He was sore from the long walk the day before and from the terrible night. He was disappointed about the weather but glad it was the morning and light and that he was out of the night tunnel. Time to head for home.

But where was home? He didn't have a map or a compass or a clue about which direction he should head in. Well, he had all day to figure it out. And people were probably looking for him too.

Chuck put on his snowshoes and slipped the backpack over his shoulders. The candy bars were gone and so was his water. He had eaten some snow when he got up, but the cold made his stomach ache.

Each step was a chore in the deep, soft snow. But he kept moving, hoping he was headed in the right direction.

He tried not to think about how worried every-one had to be. If his night was hard, how hard must it have been for his parents, he wondered, biting his lip and wishing it were food.

After a few hours, he came to a creek. Most of it was buried under a layer of ice and snow, but the water was flowing underneath. Chuck took the water bottle from his pack and walked over to the edge. He knelt on an icy rock and leaned in to fill the bottle. Suddenly, he lost his balance and fell. His right leg was in the creek, the shockingly cold creek, up to mid-thigh and when he tried to pull himself up he found that the snowshoe was snagged on something under the water.

Chuck pulled and pushed off several times, but it was no use. Finally, he reached down with his right hand to loosen the straps. His glove didn't let him get a good grip, so he took it off and plunged his arm down again into the icy depths.

He got the snowshoe off and pulled himself up. He crawled away from the water and removed the other one. His fingers were red and stinging. He blew on them and then rubbed his numb leg. Then he started running in place to try to get warm. After a few minutes the feeling came back and then the pain, a terrible burning pain. Chuck kept running and then he remembered something. He had to fish out the submerged snowshoe. He went back to the water.

Horror-struck, Chuck didn't see it. He was sure he was looking in the spot where it had been. But it wasn't there. It wasn't there! The current must have freed and taken it. Chuck started looking down the length of the creek, but the snowshoe wasn't there. It was gone.

How was he going to get back now? He started to panic and ran and stumbled up and down the shore, scanning the water with large, insane, dancing eyes.

"Not here," he shouted. "Not here!"

Chuck tried walking with one snowshoe but all that got him was an aching hip from sinking one leg deep in the snow and pulling it back out. It was no good.

Breathing hard, he sat down by a tree and smiled when the thought hit him. He would make a snowshoe. Just like people in these woods have made for hundreds and hundreds of years. He started gathering material for it as the snow finally stopped falling. A patch of blue opened up in the cloud cover.

"Maybe that's a good sign," he said, looking at the sky.

He worked for what must have been several hours on the project, not aware of the time going by. He bent and weaved the branches just so and weaved and bent some more. He used some of the backpack straps to fasten it to his boot. Finally, it was finished.

He tried it on and was impressed with how good it looked. But after a few steps, the shoe fell apart. Chuck cursed and slammed the pieces into a nearby tree trunk.

He sat down and thought about how he was focused on the wrong thing. He was trying to make the snowshoe too pretty. All it had to do was hold him up in the snow, not win some beauty contest. He started again.

He used one strap to hold several branches together and another to tie them to his boot. Better, Chuck thought. Much better!

He smiled, and even though he realized he would be spending another night out here–the sun was going down again–he felt good about his chances. Tomorrow he would make it home.

"Tomorrow," he whispered.

***

The wind became even stronger as the first rain drops fell. They were big and fat and came at him at an angle. Jacob backed away from the shore and took shelter under a pine tree. The water hit the lake in sheets and he could not see the kayak anymore. He hunkered down and wondered if he would have to spend the night out here.

Even in good weather it would take most of the day to walk through the thick brush to the other side of the lake. Except for the portages, there were no trails around these lakes. The lakes and rivers themselves *were* the trails. And it sure wasn't good weather. And it was already late afternoon. The summer sun wouldn't be going down for several hours, but in the forest it always seemed to get dark much earlier. And even if he reached the kayak as the last rays of light were leaving the sky, what then? He wouldn't paddle back in the dark.

Jacob wasn't even sure where *back* was.

***

The second night was a little easier. Easier because he had done it before and because he was so tired and was able to sleep a little more. But because it was clear, it was colder. Much colder. He had to work much harder to keep the cold away.

In the morning Chuck felt weak and sick. Whether from the cold or a fever or exhaustion, chills shot through him. He hadn't eaten anything since Monday afternoon. It was now Wednesday. He tried to count the hours but couldn't get his mind to focus.

"Had the last of the chocolate at about two that afternoon and it's now maybe eight," he said, tracing his finger around an imaginary clock while his mind started to wander.

"Had the last of the chocolate at about two that afternoon and it's now . . . "

He couldn't do it. It didn't matter anyway. How would knowing help or change anything? Would it change the size of the empty pit in his stomach or his energy level?

He strapped on the mismatched snowshoes and started off. Again, he didn't know where. But the sun was out and it rises in the east, Chuck thought, so if that's east then that must be west. His home was west, he was sure.

He kept the sun at his back and stumbled through the deep snow. The hours went by and Chuck slowed, growing weaker and weaker with each feeble step. At some point his homemade snowshoe fell apart and he sat down under a tree. And at some point the snow began falling again. Looking out, Chuck thought it was all so lovely.

"That's just beautiful," he mumbled. "Just beautiful. Wish I had a camera."

When it got dark, he didn't bother to dig a snow shelter. He just sat there.

Chuck heard the snowmobiles the next day and knew it wouldn't be long before they found him. Help was on the way and he smiled weakly and waited.

"Over here," he whispered.

***

The intensity of the storm died away. The wind diminished into a light breeze and the rain became a mist. One end of an amazing rainbow bowed down on the far end of the lake. The yellow kayak was nowhere in sight.

Jacob had to go to the bathroom. He had no toilet paper so he would have to use leaves. He wished he knew what poison ivy looked like so he could avoid it. He walked deeper into the wet woods and found a sharp rock to dig a hole. He crouched down and did his business and covered up the hole, placing the rock on top. Just then a bright flash lit up the forest followed by a thunderclap that sounded like eight pianos falling off a tall building.

Frightened, Jacob started running back toward shore. He tripped on a tree stump and fell down onto the muddy ground. He was dirty and mad–mad at himself for acting like such a baby–but unhurt.

"Get a grip, fool," he said, picking himself up.

It was then that he saw it. It looked like a large animal carcass. It was curled up like a dog. But it wasn't a dog. Looking closer, he saw the clothes. It was human. A boy, Jacob thought, but he couldn't be sure. Maybe a boy about his age.

He had been dead for a long time. The body was like something out of *C.S.I.* Except it was right here and real. A camera with a large zoom lens hung down from around the neck. In places, grayish-white bone stuck out through the decayed flesh. A large, black worm slithered out of the corner of the open mouth.

"Aaaaaah!"

Jacob started running again. He ran in no particular direction. Just ran far away from that place of horror and death.

Out of breath, he finally stopped. Regaining his senses, he tried to think where the shore would be. Everything looked the same. Then he remembered he had slipped the compass into his pants pocket. He tried to picture what the lake had looked like and where north would be and if *that* was north then, yes, the left shore of the lake, where his pack was, should be *that* way. He walked off in that direction, dodging the image of what he had just seen as it replayed and repeated in his mind.

After a few minutes the trees opened up and the lake reappeared. He soon found his pack and paddle and felt a little bit of confidence return. At least he did this, he thought. Maybe he could use the same skills to find his way back all the way.

There was no point staying here and waiting for the darkness to close in. The kayak wasn't coming back anytime soon. He figured that the portage trail that brought him to this lake was less than a mile behind him. If he stayed close to shore, it would be fairly easy to find. Then he could take it back to the other lake. Maybe his parents would be looking for him already. Maybe someone else would come along that could help him.

As he walked he thought about the dead boy. He wondered what had happened to him. How he got to be out here. How no one had found him until now. Until it was too late. And how it had been too late for a long time.

The trail was muddy, slippery, and steep in places and for a moment Jacob felt glad he didn't have to carry the kayak back down this portage. The wind and rain had finally stopped and the sky had even turned a deep shade of blue. It would be dark soon. But that was okay, he thought. He was alive. And that counted for something. That counted for a lot.

Jacob walked slowly toward the other lake and after a while the trees gave way to water. He reached the shore and scanned the horizon.

At first he didn't see anything. And then, like something out of a dream, it was there. In the distance a green canoe cut through the water. The paddlers meant business, powerfully churning the water with every stroke. Jacob could barely make out his mom's Red Sox cap riding high in the bow. His eyes watered over and a large lump grew in his throat.

They would soon all be together. And it didn't matter how mad they were. Didn't matter the least little bit. They would soon all be together.

***

Chuck hadn't heard the sound of the snowmobiles for a long time. He couldn't understand where they had gone. It didn't matter. There was no hurry now. He wasn't hungry anymore. Didn't even really feel the cold either. He slept mostly and, with what little mental energy he had left, thought about the things his grandfather had said and hoped he wouldn't be too disappointed in him for not making it. Hoped he wouldn't cry too much.

He wished he could somehow live through this and grow up and live his life. He would live it by the old code he had heard about all those times in the darkroom. Chuck wasn't sure what it meant exactly, but the way his grandfather said it, it sounded good and true and something worth shooting for.

Something worth dreaming about . . .

Acknowledgements

Much love and many thanks to Wendy, Cassandra, and Megan for coming along on this nutty ride and for their invaluable contributions toward making this book a reality.

About the Author

Under the pen name O. Penn-Coughin, Joseph Kehoe is also the author of *They're Coming For You: Scary Stories that Scream to be Read*. He lives in Bend, Oregon with his wife, two daughters, and one crazy cat. Learn more at **KehoeBooks.com**.

Writing is hard. Being in the wilderness is hard. Writing in the wilderness is real hard. Umkay?